CW00726308

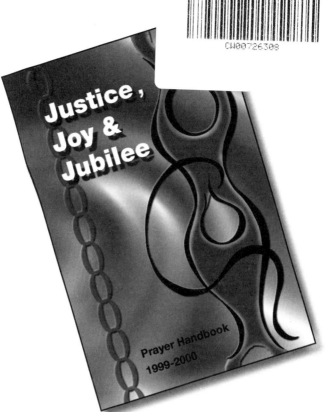

Justice,
Joy &
Jubilee

Prayer Handbook
1999-2000

Contributors

**Chris Campbell, Ed Cox, Colin Ferguson,
Melanie Frew, Nicola Furley-Smith,
Rebecca Latham, Janet Lees, Tim Lowe,
Clare McBeath, Alan Paterson,
Becky Slow, Andrew Stuart, Jill Thornton**

Editor

Janet Lees

Editorial

This year's book has been produced by a group of contributors, both writers and artists (see page 138). The theme is 'Jubilee'. The material tries to wrestle with the hope that the year 2000 will be a Jubilee but also acknowledges that much still needs to be done to bring that hope to reality. Once again the Revised Common Lectionary (year B) is used and as usual we try to pray with our partners in the Council for World Mission. We have other partners too and whilst it is difficult to include them all, we hope that what is presented here will inform and enliven our prayers beyond this particular year. We hope you will experiment with different ways of presenting these prayers in worship. Often several voices can be used rather than just one. Visual or sound accompaniment can add another dimension to our praying.

My thanks to all who took part in the process and its ups and downs. The publication of this book sees Ioan Gryffudd from the Union of Welsh Independents leave the committee after several years of service. We thank him for what he has contributed and look forward to welcoming his successor.

Janet Lees

Seven Days of Prayer -
Seven Stages of Human Development

As last year, each day of the week offers us an opportunity to consider a different stage or phase of human development. As the weeks go by this pattern will develop into a cycle of human being from beginning to ending and round again. This year the week begins with Monday as day one, and ends with Sunday as day seven when we are invited to 'celebrate'.

Read: a number of bible readings are suggested for each day.

Think: about how this bible reading relates to the experience of life for the world's poor, for example those who are living in the heavily indebted countries which feature in the book, at this particular stage in their lives.

Pray: two alternative prayers are offered.

Link: some of the other prayers in the book which links to the theme are given.

There are many ways of reflecting of the theme for the day and those listed are not meant to suggest them all, or all be done every day. You might like to collect images relevant to each life style during in the year and use these from time to time in a worship centre or quiet space. Information about Jubilee 2000 is available from Jubilee 2000 Coalition, 1 Rivington Street, London EC2A 3DT (020 773 91000; www.jubilee2000.uk.org).

The Jubilee Gloria could be used as a closing prayer for any day:

Jubilee Gloria

Glory to the Holy One, God of Jubilee:
dancing through the cosmos,
a partnership of three;
Creator, Son and Spirit, bringing all to be;
glory, glory, glory, God of Jubilee.

Monday, day one   Life Stage: Baby
Theme: Beginning

Read any one of the following
Genesis 29.31-35; Exodus 1.15-17; Exodus 2.1-2; Ruth 4.16-17;
1Sam 4.20-22; 2 Sam 12.15b-19; 2 Sam 14.25; Psalm 139.13-14;
Isaiah 9.6; Isaiah 49.15; Luke 2.6-7; John 1.12-13; John 9.1-3;
1 Cor 1.26.

Think   What does the chosen text say to you about being a baby?
Reflect on images of babies you recall or have collected, from
different circumstances worldwide. Look up stories about babies
in this book on pages 17,37 and 81.

Pray
Dear God, for jubilee I would like.....
a new beginning with you,
a new beginning in my relationships,
a new beginning for the poor of the world.
[add any new beginning you wish]

or   God of beginnings,
                     here we can all begin again:
                     with you, with each other,
                     with the poor, who are always with us.
                     Help me to see the marks
                     of your new start in us and around us today.

Link   Christmas Day, Lent 2 and 13 after Pentecost.

Tuesday, day two   Life Stage: Toddler
Theme: Exploring

Read any one of the following
Exodus 1.9-10; 1 Sam 1.27-28; 1 Kings 3.27; Isaiah 11.6;
Isaiah 11.8-9; Isaiah 40.11; Isaiah 43.5-6; Isaiah 49.22;
Hosea 11.1,3; Micah 2.9; Malachi 4.6; Matthew 2.16-18;
Matthew 19.13-15; Luke 2.22.

Think What does the chosen text say to you about being a toddler? Reflect on images of toddlers you recall or have collected, from different circumstances worldwide. Look up stories about toddlers in this book on pages 79 and 109.

Pray
Dear God, for jubilee I would like.....
to explore new ways of praying,
to explore new ideas,
to explore new places.
[add anything you want to explore]

or   Travelling Christ,
        I get the message that you want me to keep looking,
        to keep moving on.
        I need your company to cope with my preference for the past,
        to show me the signs of promise in the present.
        May the Spirit's energy coax me to explore a bit further today.

Link   Christmas 2, Easter 3, 15 after Pentecost.

Wednesday, day three   Life Stage: Child
Theme: Growing

Read any one of the following
1 Sam 2.21; 1 Sam 3.10; 1 Sam 16.19-21; 1 Sam 20.35-40;
2 Sam 4.4; Jeremiah 1.6-7; Mark 9.17-18; Luke 1.80; Luke 2.40;
John 6.8-9; Acts 16.16-18; Romans 8.14; 1 Cor 12.27; 1 Cor 13.11;
2 Cor 11-13; Phil 2.5-7.

Think What does the chosen text say to you about being a child? Reflect on images of children you recall or have collected, from different circumstances worldwide. Look up stories about children in this book on pages 79, 85, 97 and 123.

Pray
Dear God, for jubilee I would like.....
to grow in faith, hope and love,
to help others to grow,
for your Church to grow.
[add anything you want to grow]

or   Sometimes growth is slow and I ache to move it on.
         Sometimes growth is quick and it overwhelms me.
         God of growth, help me keep pace
         with growth in your time.

Link   Advent 3, Epiphany 2, Trinity, 14 and 17 after Pentecost.

Thursday, day four   Life Stage: Teenager
Theme: Challenging

Read any one of the following
Isaiah 40.30-31; Matthew 9.23-26; Mark 7.26-28; Mark 10.20-22;
Luke 2.46-47; John 1.43-46; John 4.27-29; John 6.66-67; John
9.20-21; John 20.24-25; Acts 12.12-15; Acts 26.1; Romans 16.3.

Think What does the chosen text say to you about being a
teenager? Reflect on images of teenagers you recall or have
collected, from different circumstances worldwide. Look up stories
about teenagers in this book on pages 31,109 and 119.

Pray
Dear God, for jubilee I would like.....
to be challenged by you,
to be challenged for mission,
to be challenged by the poor or the world.
[add any challenges you want to name]

or   Challenging God,
         you keep nudging me,
         sometimes in big ways, sometimes in small ones.
         Your challenges come to me through
         people around me and through the poor of the world.
         Thanks for the challenges which cause me to reconsider
         comfortable patterns,
         and for the grace to keep exploring.

Link   Advent 2, 4,9 and 22 after Pentecost.

Friday, day five   Life Stage: Young Adult
Theme: Generating

Read any one of the following
Isaiah 66.7; Matthew 1.20-21; Matthew 20.20-22a; Luke 1.24-25,
Luke 1.30, 38; Luke 4.14-15; Luke 5.27-28; Luke 11.11-13;
John 12.24; John 15.1-2; Acts 1.26; Acts 8.30-31; Acts 16.32-34;
Romans 16.1-2.

Think   What does the chosen text say to you about being a
young adult? Reflect on images of young adults you recall or have
collected, from different circumstances worldwide. Look up stories
about young adults in this book on pages 33, 37, 57, 58-59 and 105.

Pray
Dear God, for jubilee I would like.....
to create a healthy way of living,
to make a contribution to the poor of the world,
to make a fruitful contribution to your Church.
[add anything you want to create, make or produce]

or   Creator God,
         may my contribution to the created order
         make a difference to the situations I encounter today.
         May the Spirit's enthusiasm inspire me to
         devote my energy to building a healthy community.

Link   Advent 4, Lent 1, Easter 5, 7 after Pentecost.

Saturday, day six   Life Stage: Mature Adult
Theme: Sustaining

Read any one of the following
Joel 2.28; Matthew 2.13-15; Matthew 12.46-50; Mark 1.12-13;
Mark 14.37-38; Mark 15.21; Luke 8.1-3; Luke 9.61-62;
Luke 10.38-39; Luke 21.1-4; John 8.10-11; John 21.15;
Acts 4.21-22; Acts 16.40.

Think   What does the chosen text say to you about being a mature adult? Reflect on images of mature adults you recall or have collected, from different circumstances worldwide. Look up stories about mature adults in this book on pages 19, 35, 47, 87 and 115.

Pray
Dear God, for jubilee I would like.....
to maintain my relationship with you,
to confirm*the endurance of my relationships,
to support the poor of the world.
[add anything you want to maintain, sustain or support]

or   Sustaining God,
I sometimes feel I've let go at my end,
or that things are slipping through my fingers.
Help me to face up to these situations,
knowing that although you hold all things together,
you also know how to let go.
May the give and take of the Spirit's breath
inspire me to take a fresh hold on life today.

Link   Epiphany 3 and 6, Lent 3, Ascension,
10 and 12 after Pentecost.

Sunday, day seven   Life Stage: Third Age/Retirement
Theme: Celebrating

Read any one of the following
Isaiah 46.3-4; Matthew 26.10-13; Mark 1.40-45; Mark 10.29-31;
Luke 1.21-23; Luke 1.67-68; Luke 2.28-32; Luke 2.36-38; Luke 7.11-13; Luke 15.8-9; John 11.32-35; Acts 1.46-47; Acts 28.30-31; Romans 16.25-27; 1 Cor 11.23-26; Phil 4.4-7.

Think   What does the chosen text say to you about being an elderly person? Reflect on images of elderly people you recall or have collected, from different circumstances worldwide. Look up stories about elderly people in this book on pages 95, 111 and 129.

6

Pray
Dear God, for jubilee I would like.....
to celebrate my relationship with you,
to celebrate the fun of faith with my friends,
to celebrate with the poor of the world.
[add anything you want to celebrate]

or   God of Jubilee
there's much to celebrate:
whether it's with loud sounds or silent reflections.
I look forward to celebrating all of today with you,
with those close to me
and those far away.
May the riotous Spirit, who can also move so silently,
fill all our Jubilee celebrations.

Link   Christmas 1, New Year, 2, 5 and 20 after Pentecost.

More daily prayer resources are available at
http:/www.bobjanet.demon.co.uk/prytoday.html

Read · **Isaiah 64.1-9; Psalm 80.1-7, 17-19**

A day, an hour, no-one knows...
the sun darkened under clouds of pollution;
the moon trampled on, despoiled of her mystery;
missiles in the guise of stars rain from the skies;
the earth quakes with the wrenching sobs of grief...

How long O Lord? How long?
How long will you hide your face from us?
How long will you feed us with the bread of tears?
How long will our oppressors laugh among themselves?

Forgive us for our complicity in the devastation of the
earth and her peoples,
Forgive us for our complacency in the face of your
children's suffering.
Restore us O Lord,
that we may reflect the light of your justice
to the ends of the earth.

Music for Declare the Year of Jubilee!

E. Cox (harm. M. Scott) 1999

Declare the year of Jubilee!

(Based on Leviticus 25 / Luke 4)

Sound the trumpet!
Sound the horn!
Declare the year of Jubilee!
Let's celebrate with songs of hope
Of living, loving unity.

Bang the timbral!
Stamp the ground!
Declare the year of Jubilee!
Let's demonstrate with shouts of 'No'
to modern forms of slavery.

Strum the harp!
Pluck the lyre!
Declare the year of Jubilee!
Let's weep together, you and I,
and seek again God's sovereignty.

Sound the trumpet!
Sound the horn!
Declare the year of Jubilee!
Let's celebrate with songs of joy
for Christ the Lord has set us free.

The Tear

(Based on Psalm 80)

A bright silver tear
- like a fairground balloon
waiting to burst -
welled up in the eye of injustice.

A momentary blink
tipped it over the edge,
spilling bittersweet saltiness
down the cheek of time.

Charting its glistening path
across dry tender skin,
it paused ... as if to ponder
new found freedom.

And as it perched
it was swept away
by a gentle hand:
the promise of a new future.

9

Read	**Isaiah 40.1-11**

Voice 1   *A voice cries out:*
'In the wilderness, prepare the way of the Lord!'

Voice 2   God of the highways and byways,
As we journey towards the end of the millennium
make our paths straight
and provide for us a broad carriageway of opportunities
through the narrow gate of your kingdom
and into the new century.

Voice 1   *A voice says: 'Cry out!'*
And I said 'What shall I cry?'

Voice 2   God of grass and flower,
As the twentieth century withers and fades
may your word stand forever.
We are surrounded by clanging cymbals:
reviews and perspectives,
prophecies and promises,
manifestos and mission statements for the new millennium,
festivity and folly.
Show us what we are to cry,
speak to us in that still small voice,
stir us to shout: 'Here is your God!'.

Voice 1   *A voice says:*
'Comfort, O comfort my people!'

Voice 2   God of peace,
Renew us with your Spirit, our comforter,
to speak tenderly to your people,
from Jerusalem to the ends of the earth,
from today until the end of time.

An appropriate sung response may be used between stanzas, for example 'Prepare ye the way of the Lord' from Godspell.

Kissing God

(Based on Psalm 85)

Peace kisses righteousness with the soft warmth of a lover
because she knows the value of silent communication ...

Righteousness kisses peace with a shrill smacker on the cheek
because he knows her temptation to become dreamy ...

They both kiss each other with the lingering of a long goodbye
because with lips pressed together neither can say a word.

Read | **Isaiah 61.1-4, 8-11**
(New Revised Standard Version)

Voice 1   *God of justice,*
clothe us with garlands instead of ashes...

Voice 2   ashes of earth lying desolate, raped of her riches,
ashes caked to the face of a pot-bellied child,
ashes of a burnt out car, abandoned in a city street,
ashes flicked from a splif, drugs gripping lives with despair.

Adorn us in garlands of justice, joy and jubilee.

Voice 1   *God of joy,*
clothe us with garlands instead of ashes...

Voice 2   ashes and earth mingle, fertilising seeds of hope,
ashes sown with tears, springing shoots of new life,
ashes blossoming into garlands draping earth's garden,
garlands of berries jewelled with the extravagance of
harvest abundance.

Adorn us in garlands of justice, joy and jubilee.

Voice 1   *God of jubilee,*
clothe us with garlands instead of ashes,

Voice 2   garlands of paper streamers festooning a shanty town,
garlands of tinsel and glitter heralding the advent of
Christmas,
garlands of hands intertwined round a table,
garlands of celebration sounding the trumpet of jubilee.

Adorn us in garlands of justice, joy and jubilee.

Children's Jubilee Prayers

(to be read by two children's voices
reading each line alternately)

Dear God

Dear God

for Jubilee I would like ...

for Jubilee I would like ...

to have a chocolate birthday cake everyday

something good to eat today

to hold hands with a new friend

a hand to hold

to give people smiles

somewhere to play

to stop people crying about bad things

the guns to stop

to understand the whispers

everybody to hear my whispers

to sing a new song

to sing a new song

love me xx

love me xx

*Tim Lowe, Clare McBeath,
Rebekah Slow, Jill Thornton*

My soul magnifies the Lord
    and I dance with God who liberates me,
for she has remembered with love
    the whispered song of her shadow.
Surely, from now on my story will be
    handed down to all generations.
For the One who is Love
    has cradled my life in her arms
  and beautiful is her name.
Her tenderness enfolds our brokenness
    through all generations.

Her voice clamours in shouts of justice,
wrenching free the grip of the abuser.
She gathers the abused to her breast,
    her milk nurturing those who seek her,
    according to the promise given to
        our grandmothers,
    to Sarah and Hagar
        and their children forever.

Read John 1.1-14

In the beginning, your Word was in creation.
>Moving with it,
>exploding and merging, with neutrons and protons;
>swirling and spinning, with planets and stars.
>>Growing with it,
>>multiplying and replicating, with molecules and microbes;
>>reproducing and evolving, with cells and organisms.

In the world, your Son is in creation.
>Born into it,
>living and breathing, with flesh and bone;
>crying and laughing, with parents and family.
>>Serving in the world,
>>teaching and loving, with friends and enemies,
>>crucified and suffering, with blood and nails.

In him, is a sign of your forgiveness and healing;
>that you are not using the world,
>but appreciating it;
>embracing and nurturing every life.
>>Living and loving in us.
>>Smiling at us.
>>Crying with us.

In love, you continue the miracle of your creation.
>As we are born through each new sunrise
>may we see your light and hope more clearly.
>As we witness nature's beauty through each new moonrise
>may we love you more dearly, as your faithful stewards.
>That we may be alive to the wonder of the commonplace!
>For that is the gift of a wildly generous creator!

Every second, one person is born into bad, unpayable debt in the world's poorest countries.

George Carey

Where slaves were once sent with a price attached to them, now children are born with a debt around their necks. In Tanzania each new baby owes in the region of $250; in Mozambique, $350.

The New Abolitionists, Christian Aid

Believe me, no child will be born unless he is surrounded by song.
No man will die without being surrounded by song.
This is how we turn our tragedy to triumph.

Sudanese Proverb

pray with partner churches in Sudan; pray for the world's children.

Read   All

God of the generations,
> we celebrate with you in the miracle of new life,
> the wonder of the first glimpse into new-born eyes,
> the excitement of the first grasp of tiny fingers,
> as we name the promise of future hope.

From age to age, may we grow in faith

God of the generations,
> we praise you for the joy and pain of parenting,
> from the thrill of first footsteps, to the worry of leaving home,
> from the tears of teething, to the celebration of the first kiss,
> nurture us as we nurture the children in our lives.

From age to age, may we grow in faith

God of the generations,
> we come as heirs to your kingdom,
> standing on the shoulders of past generations,
> excited by the challenge set before us,
> yet humbled by your faith in us.

From age to age, may we grow in faith.

Eastern tradition is to be acknowledged; wisdom should be considered as the gift of years, not of youth. I claim Advent and Christmas as a time for adults; not out of any dislike for children, but because I fear that by viewing these seasons as if they were devoted to and for toddlers, we avoid one of the quirks of God's nature. God expects old dogs to do new tricks.

John Bell

All-age church
What is an all-age church ? How would you define it ?
Does it need to have people from every age band in it - or is it more about attitudes ?
Ask the group to bring a recent photo of themselves. Underneath the photo invite people to write what they think an all-age church might be by completing the phrase 'An all-age church is......' Put all of the photographs and ideas together on one board at the entrance to your church for this week.

pray for your 'all-age' community of faith and for partner churches in Wales and Scotland.

The idea behind this is really just for a bit of fun and to remind us that God is present throughout time, not just in what we think are the significant moments. It is also a reminder that we are called to work for justice and jubilee throughout the year and not just at the beginning of a new millennium. It is suggested that 12 chimes could be sounded at the start of the prayer - or twelve party poppers - or use these as part of a prayer activity.

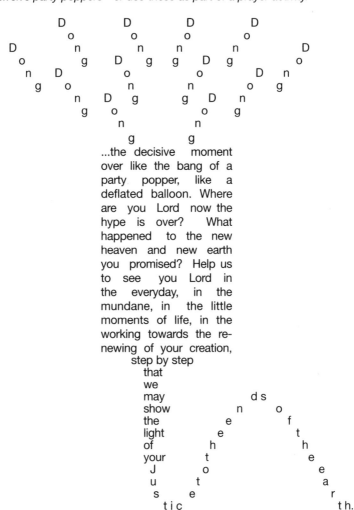

```
            D           D           D           D
               o           o           o           o
    D             n           n           n             D
      o        g   D   g   g   D   g                 o
        n   D         o           o           D   n
     g   o           n           n           o   g
          n     D   g         g   D   n
            g     o             o   g
                n               n
                g               g
```

...the decisive moment over like the bang of a party popper, like a deflated balloon. Where are you Lord now the hype is over? What happened to the new heaven and new earth you promised? Help us to see you Lord in the everyday, in the mundane, in the little moments of life, in the working towards the renewing of your creation, step by step

```
                    that
                    we
                    may                d s
                    show            n      o
                    the          e           f
                    light      e              t
                    of        h               h
                    your      t                 e
                    J        o                   e
                    u        t                   a
                    s        e                   r
                      t i c                      t h.
```

Time for Justice

(Based on Ecclesiastes 3.1-13)

Like the smell of the harvest field,
the spring flower, the coal fire, the freshly mown lawn,
your seasons grow and die without tears.
Teach us to stand still
and taste the joy of now-being.

Like the shadows cast by standing stones
you bear witness to the endurance of history.
May we never forget those ancestors and traditions
which inhabit our innermost beings.

Like the rush and push of hourglass sand
your opportunities slip swiftly into dust.
Help us to grasp each precious minute
with the love that lasts a lifetime.

Like the ticking of the classroom clock
your every moment lasts an eternity.
Be with us in the waiting time,
as we sit with those who suffer.

Like the beating of a lover's heart
the pulse of your Spirit pounds with excitement.
Arouse us from our lazy resting places
to keep pace with our busy world.

Like the chiming of the midnight bell
you ring out the old and ring in the new.
Celebrate with us this happy day
that tomorrow there will be jubilee.

Ed Cox

pray with partners in Kiribati, and others in the Pacific
Region of CWM; first with the sunrise of the new millennium.

Read   Psalm 8

identity imprinted in tiny fingers
    cradled in the womb

sticky hands falteringly discovering
    the textures of earth

fists clenched, fingers clinging, not in hate,
    but searching for security

hands 'imperfectly' formed, their beauty
    challenging perceptions of perfection

fleshy skin in a myriad of tones,
    brimming with creative possibility

Closing Prayer
Read Galatians 4.4-7

Child-like God,
    - make us restless, full of energy
        to do the work of your kingdom,
    - make us playful, full of the vibrant
        joy of life,
    - make us vulnerable, sensitive to the
        pain and need of others,
    - make us indignant, fired up with justice
        for a fairer world,
in the name of Jesus,
    the child of Nazareth.

Blessing
Read **Numbers 6.22-27**

May the blessing of the child-like God be with you,
May the blessing of the child of Nazareth be with you,
May the blessing of the Spirit who names us
as children of God, be with you.

The Flower

God looks into my eyes
as a child looks at a flower.

You are beautiful and small.
You are tenderly made fragile.
Your colours delight and confuse.

And so God touches me gently.
For though I am weak, small and confusing,
God's world would be less colourful without me.

Ed Cox

Read   Isaiah 60.1-6

Lord of the dawn,
where your people live in darkness
let your light sweep in.

Lord of the noon,
where your people are dazzled by evil
let you light sweep in.

Lord of the evening,
where your people fear the night
let your light sweep in.

Lord of the night,
where your people pray for morning
let your light sweep in

Lord of our lives,
As we grow into a new year of hopes and possibilities
let your light sweep in.

.. they went home by another route.

'We went home. Three ordinary women. We lived our lives. Some called us wise because of the way we tried to answer many questions. We think it would be more honest to say we were amazed. The three amazed women. For we were amazed that we should see God. But we did and we're not afraid to say so.'

Janet Lees

Change the debt rules

Debt is everywhere a feature of our lives. Debt is found throughout human history and in every society. The acceptable face of debt is credit - loans for cars and houses in Britain for example, or microcredit in Bangladesh. But debt can also abuse and exploit, as with loan sharks in Britain and with debt of poor countries to rich countries.

Poverty in the developing world was not caused by debt, but the growing burden on poor countries perpetuates and increases poverty. Debt repayments divert scarce resources away from basic service like health, education and infrastructure.

'The Group of Eight' represents the richest and most powerful countries on earth: Canada, France, Germany, Italy, Japan, Russia, UK and USA. To contrast with the G8, Christian Aid has focused on eight much poorer and heavily-indebted countries: Bangladesh, Bolivia, Ethiopia, Jamaica, Nicaragua, Malawi, Mozambique and Tanzania, from each continent of the South.

Forever in your Debt: eight poor nations and the G8

During the eight weeks of Epiphany we will think about these 8 poor countries. Begin now by asking yourself how much do you know about them. Over the eight weeks look at how often are they in the news and why. Try to find out something of what is happening in these countries and the lives of the people who live in them. Look in the middle section to see what our partner CWM churches are doing in some of these countries. We will revisit these countries in the first few weeks after Easter.

Note, to compare UK with these 8 poor countries this information is provided by Christian Aid

- 99% for women or men can read and write;
- life expectancy is 79 years for women and 74 years for men, on average;
- 10,000 children die before their first birthday every year.

Read   **Acts 19.1-9; Mark 1.4-11**

We are hiding.
We are hiding from your first-day-light
and your voice of thunder.
We are hiding behind traditions;
weíve always done it this way.
Weíre hiding in the past;
it was so much better then.
Weíre hiding our prejudice;
welcoming only those who mirror our behaviour and attitudes.
We are hiding.

But just as the people of Ephesus had to answer Paulís questions,
we too have to respond honestly.
We have forgotten the small, most important stories:
when the Holy Spirit came to the twelve it came when they were
most vulnerable.
We will no longer hide behind these masks.
We will make the ultimate sacrifice;
to live the life you want us to live,
as your own dear ones.

Ethiopian Environmental Non-Governmental Organisation (EENGO) was established in 1992 to work with small farmers on environmental protection and rehabilitation. They aim to:
- promote tree planting
- train farmers in soil and water conservation and afforestation
- train women in the production and use of fuel-wood saving stoves
- assist farmers in sustainable agriculture
- construct hand-dug wells and spring developments and rural town water supplies.

For example, the new pump at Arkissa village, built and installed at EENGO in 1996 supplies about 420 people in 60 households. Four people have been trained to maintain the pump. The village people say that having clean water has reduced stomach complaints and everyone's health is much improved.

Faith Atlas: Africa

In Ethiopia today
- 24% of women and 44% of men can read and write;
- 625,000 children a year die before reaching their first birthday;
- 25% of people have access to safe water.

Forever in your Debt: eight poor nations and the G8

pray with partner churches in Ethiopia, and for environmental projects for agriculture and water supplies.

Read   1 Samuel 3.1-10; Psalm 139.1-6, 13-18

Here I am
> Here in my life;
> busy being busy,
> busy being me.

For you called me
> Called me by my name;
> all I am,
> all I'll be.

I am listening
> Listening for your word;
> when I'm not too busy,
> or thinking of myself.

You searched me and know me
> Laid open my thoughts to you;
> let you in,
> dwelling in my life.

Lay your hand upon me
> The hand that formed my bones;
> cradled me then,
> cradle me now.

You are still with me
> I will stay with you;
> despite myself,
> despite my ways.

We are here, called by you and listening to you.
Help us to know and cradle your creation
as you know and cradle us.

Here I am

'I would ask people in your country not to forget us here in Bolivia, to think about what is going on. Really, it seems to me that a lot of the people in richer countries don't care about poor countries like Bolivia, they only seem to care about themselves or their nearest neighbours. It really surprises me to hear about this campaign (Jubilee 2000) which you are launching about our foreign debt - that people so far away are interested in forgotten people like us'.

Bolivia is another example of how Western creditor lent vast sums to obviously corrupt regimes. By the time of return to civilian government (from 11 years of military government) in 1982, Bolivia's debt had reached $3.6 billion, an increase of more than 400%. The military officials left office with most of this lending in their pockets.

In Bolivia today
- 36,000 children a year die before their first birthday;
- 19.6. per cent of the population are not expected to live to the age of 40 years;
- the adult literacy rates are 75.2% for women and 90.4 % for men.

Forever in your Debt: eight poor nations and the G8

pray with partner churches in Bolivia, for community education and health projects.

Should I wear sackcloth for the smile I did not smile,
the patience I did not show,
the need I turned my back on,
the love that I still owe?
Forgive me and help me to do better next time...

Should I fast to atone for the advice that I resented,
the person whom I ignored,
the anger I have inside me,
the counsel I withhold?
Forgive me and help me to do better next time...

Should I pay penance for the sin I can't confess,
The prayer I left unsaid,
the self that I put first,
the God I leave aside?
Forgive me and help me to do better next time...

Should I accept that the joy that you give,
the love that you show,
the truth that you bring,
is all the forgiveness I need?
Forgive me and help me to do better next time...

Employment of children under 14 permeates the economies of most developing nations. But most of the children work in small local industries. In Bangladesh, this means only 4% of working children work in firms susceptible to foreign boycotts. Sometimes earning money alongside their parents, they are paid pitifully low wages for breaking bricks, collecting minibus fares or sorting rubbish, for example. On the crowded Bruinga river in Dhaka, young boys are employed to clean and refill old oil drums all day long at the muddy water's edge. Their legs marked by ulcerating sores, they stack, scrub down and repair the massive drums. "If I go to school, how will I eat. Who will pay the rent money if I don't work".
Iqbal, aged 10 years.

"I work from 7am to 9am and from 7pm to 8pm in the evening after school. My father is a rickshaw puller and he couldn't afford to send me to school before now".
Shajeda, 15 years old, who makes incense sticks.   *The Guardian*

Hafeeza is 14 years old and has 8 siblings. Before Hafeeza could read or write she didn't know about savings and looking after poultry, but now she is very wise. Eighteen months ago she purchased a goat for 200 Taka (about £3) and from this she bred 10 goats, which she sold for 3000 Taka. Now she has just one goat and had invested money in tree planting. To date she has planted 50 guava trees, 10 coconut trees and 50 others. She now has 15 chickens and 12 geese. She is now teaching 7 other village children to read.
Faith Atlas: Bangladesh

In Bangladesh today
• 24% of women and 48% of men can read and write;
• 537,000 children a year die before they are a year old;
• 45% of the population have access to health services;
UNICEF estimates that there are 250 million child labourers in the world.

pray with partner churches in Bangladesh, and work by UNICEF and others concerned about child labour.

Read **Psalm 111**

My eyes praise the Lord!
Look how wonderful God is.
My stomach praises the Lord!
Look how generous God is.
My hands praise the Lord!
Look how gentle God is.

My mouth praises the Lord!
I will worship God forever.
My lungs praise the Lord!
May God's Spirit fill me.
My shoulders praise the Lord!
I will bear God's yoke each day.

My heart praises the Lord!
Its regular beat reminds me of God's promises
My knees praise the Lord!
I bend to and offer my whole self
My feet praise the Lord!
I stand on holy ground.

"There can be no daily democracy without daily citizenship".

Ralph Nader

In Malawi, a country which only recently emerged from a dictatorship, Christian Aid supports the work of the Public Affairs Committee (PAC) which is working through local churches and mosques to promote democratic practices and to educate the electorate at community level about their rights and responsibilities. PAC has a vital role in monitoring elections for fraud and has been very vocal in publicly denouncing the two-year postponement of local elections which limits people's capacity to participate in the democratic process on a regional level.

In Malawi today
- 40% of women and 72% of men can read and write;
- 142,000 children a year die before their first birthday;
- only 6% of the population have access to safe sanitation;

Forever in your Debt: eight poor nations and the G8

 pray with partner churches in Malawi, and for community based worked in electoral education.

Read   Isaiah 40.21- 31

Trapped by the violence of someone once loved;
held by the poverty of a crop dried up;
threatened by the state for views strongly held.
> *Those who wait on the Lord shall renew their strength*
> *They shall mount up with wings like eagles.*

Imprisoned at home by the fear of outside;
frozen by the frost on the street at night;
lost in a maze of benefit claims.
> *Those who wait on the Lord shall renew their strength*
> *They shall mount up with wings like eagles.*

Chained to the concrete of a protest tunnel;
victimised by those who see in black and white;
excluded by society's dis-ability to change.
> *Those who wait on the Lord shall renew their strength*
> *They shall mount up with wings like eagles.*

Abused by a friend whom they thought they could trust;
oppressed by the dark blanket of depression;
consumed by the fear of playground bullies.
> *Those who wait on the Lord shall renew their strength*
> *They shall mount up with wings like eagles.*

Everlasting God, we hear your promise to us.
> Thank you for your support when we are weary,
> for your strength when we are faint.
> Uphold us and embrace us with your power.

Agnes looks to be in her late 50s, but it is difficult to tell. She could be much younger; 16 years of bloody civil war in which her eldest daughter was killed, and the long painful process of trying to rebuild her life since the peace accord was signed in 1992 have etched deep lines of pain and weariness on her face. Agnes lives in a part of eastern Mozambique which saw some of the fiercest fighting. During the war, tens of thousands of people fled. Roads, bridges, shops, schools and hospitals were destroyed either by explosives or by a decade of sheer neglect. With little remaining intact and their houses destroyed, Agnes and her neighbours have to start from scratch. As a widow bringing up three children alone, Agnes represents one of the very poorest sectors of this economically marginalised region. Agnes dreams of her own bicycle, but the only ones in the village belong to men. Her son-in-law has a bicycle and offers to take some of her produce to sell in Malawi which is over three days cycle ride away.

Mozambique today....
- is one of the most aid dependant countries in the world;
- only 22% of women can read and write;
- 171,000 children a year die before their first birthday;
- only 63% of the population have access to safe water.

Forever in your Debt: eight poor nations and the G8

Silence is not a level playing field.

Just like debt, silence is not a level playing field either.

To increase your understanding of the different kinds of silence, in a group, or alone, think of the following:
- a time I was silent
- a time I was silenced
- a time I spoke out
- a time I was empowered to speak.

Try to be aware of those who are unable to contribute verbally, or who rarely do.

---

pray with partner churches in Mozambique, and for the ongoing CWM campaign 'Women Take Control of their Lives'.

Running the race

Under starter's orders...
> Help us to see the task ahead, Lord,
> so we do not become daunted
> and give in before we start.

They're off!
> Help us to start as we mean to go on, Lord,
> as we leave our old selves behind
> and set off on our new journey.

Dropping behind...
> Help us to keep going, Lord,
> when the work seems too much
> and we grow weary in our duties.

Head-to-head
> Help us to gain strength from others, Lord,
> when it feels as if the world is against us
> so help us to work as a team.

Home straight
> Help us to see the prize, Lord,
> when we feel so far from you
> and yet you are so near.

Victory!
> Help us proclaim your victory, Lord,
> as we must not compete for ourselves
> but for your glory alone.

Epiphany 6

From the cradle to the grave: debt and health in Tanzania

Esther is from Tanzania. She has two children; David and Joyce. During the labour with her first child, David, the health clinic in Mavala was not built, so she tried to reach the hospital in the next village which is 9 km away.

"I started to walk to the hospital but failed and came back".

Often there is no access to medical care during and after the birth of their babies, so Tanzanian women face a risk of death which is 50 times greater than women in northern Europe. However concerns for her new daughter take precedence over concerns for herself:

"I don't know whether my child will grow up and reach adulthood. She may get ill and die. There is nothing I can do about it. Some children are going to die young."

The family managed to raise the £4 fee for Joyce's delivery at the hospital. Even so, baby Joyce is 14 times more likely to die in her first year than babies born in Britain.

"People will really struggle to get the money if their child gets ill. You can't just leave your child if it is sick, can you?"

Forever in your Debt: eight poor nations and the G8

If you choose......

We can choose whether to support the people of Tanzania or not. We can choose to buy fairly traded products like tea and coffee from local producers through Traidcraft. At a worship service or meeting at your church this week choose to serve fairly traded tea or coffee from Tanzania.

---

pray for partner churches in Tanzania and the work of Traidcraft, supporting Fair Trade with Tanzania.

Read   2 Corinthians 1.18-22

Yes, Lord, you promise us -
yes to life
yes to hope
yes to joy.
Yes.

Yes but, Lord, we say to you -
yes, but it's hard
yes, but we're unsure
yes, but we haven't time.
But.

No, Lord, would be more honest -
no, we won't
no, we don't want to
no, we don't feel able.
No.

Yes, Lord, you still promise us -
yes, despite our unbelief
yes, despite our selfishness
yes, despite our reluctance.
Yes.

Yes, Lord, we do accept you -
yes thank you for your life
yes thank you for your hope
yes thank you for your joy.
Yes, Lord!

The tarmac road cuts through the zinc fencing and dust lanes of Bennett Lands, one of Kingston's downtown communities. It's a good road compared to many in the area bit it's the sort of road that the local middle classes fear to drive down after dark. On a bend in the road that the project takes its name from, the S-Corner clinic provides a range of health services, education, help with sanitation - there is no official sewerage system - and increased access to drinkable water. There is even a modest nutrition scheme encouraging local people to grow their own food for consumption and sale. But the community S-Corner serves and is a part of is not just poor and lacking amenities; it has also been riven with violence. And S-Corner has only been able to function by brokering treaties between warring factions. This is the secret of their remarkable success to date in the face of complex social problems caused by poverty.

As a lower middle-income country, Jamaica is considered too rich to qualify for debt relief under the current international initiative. But the crude statistics hide a gulf between rich and poor and a picture of harsh deprivation. Roughly one third of the population lives in absolute poverty.

In Jamaica today
"The outstanding phenomenon of Jamaica is that the country has one of the most unequally distributed incomes in the world".

UNICEF

- 88% of women and 79% of men can read and write;
- 86% of the population have access to safe water.

Forever in your Debt: eight poor nations and the G8

pray with partner churches in Jamaica and the S-Corner project.

Read   **2 Corinthians 3.1 - 6**

Let us give thanks:

> for the story of creation retold over generations;
> for the history of your people as they struggled to find your way;
> for the skill of the Gospel writers who share with us the life of
> > Jesus;
> For the letters of Paul, Peter, Jude and John who tell of your
> > Spirit in action.

Let us proclaim your glory.
Help us boast of you.

Let us give thanks:

> for the writers of children's books telling your stories in pictures;
> for today's Christian writers bringing fresh light on your word;
> for those who translate the Bible so the whole world may share
> > in the good news;
> for letters in their millions written to comfort and encourage.

Let us proclaim your glory.
Help us boast of you.

Let us give thanks:

> for news from around the world to guide our intercessions;
> for talking books and Braille when the printed page is blank;
> for the words written on our hearts forming the basis of our faith;
> for the words we use in worship to pray and praise your name.

Let us proclaim your glory.
Help us boast of you.

Nicaraguan novelist Sergio Ramirez, former vice-president of the country, wrote that since the 1972 earthquake, Nicaragua has become increasingly like Sisyphus, forced to roll an enormous rock towards the top of a hill, only for it to fall back repeatedly down to the bottom. The image is particularly appropriate. In the last 10 years, the country has been lashed by two hurricanes, its Pacific coast smashed by a tidal wave and the areas around Cerro Negro volcano have suffered two eruptions. In the midst of all the destruction however there were signs of hope. After the 1998 hurricane, in Posoltega, a six month old child was found alive and well, playing on a rock surrounded by the mud. Apparently it had been carried three kilometres from the community of El Porvenir by a mud slide. Against such an image of new life in the wake of the disaster, the traditionally resilient Nicaraguan people are preparing to start rolling the rock back up the hill. But this time, it weighs that much heavier, and the top seems that much further away.

The Guardian

In Nicaragua today
* 66% of women and 64% of men can read and write;
* 14,000 children a year die before their first birthday;
* 53% of people have access to safe water.

Forever in your Debt: eight poor nations and the G8

pray with partner churches in Nicaragua.

Read **Mark 9.3**

Show us your glory...
>the glory of your kingdom seen only in part;
>the glory of your Son at your side;
>the glory of your Spirit amongst us.

Show us your power...
>the power to forgive even the greatest sin;
>the power to heal and bring wholeness;
>the power to save us from ourselves.

Show us your love...
>the love to reach out to the neglected;
>the love to hold on when others give up;
>the love to feed us when we are empty.

Show us yourself.

Transfiguration

.... as they were coming down from the mountain;

works as a Saviour figure for me not because he went up the mountain and was transfigured there; I still have trouble with that bit. I can call Jesus Saviour and Redeemer because he came down the mountain afterwards. He didn't stay up there on a pedestal but he came down and got his hands dirty. He came down and met a poor family whose child had epilepsy and who couldn't afford medical care, and he got right to the heart of their need. So don't stand there gawping at the mountain or sighing at the sight of heaven, get on down here in the dust and dirt of daily life and attend to the needs of God's people wherever you are, and then see if you understand salvation and redemption and Jesus any better.

Spending a whole year thinking about very poor countries could be a depressing experience. When we pray we often look for something uplifting and affirming. Too much debt and poverty, problems too big to solve might all become rather a turn-off in Jubilee year. Then come down off your mountain. Leave behind the dazzling experience of lofty holiness and be prepared to be changed by the dirt and the debt that has been changing the lives of millions of people throughout the world - our neighbours. Prayer changes: high or low it can change us as well as hold out the hope of change for those neighbours. But only if we are prepared to stick at it, through the difficult bits as well as the exciting bits. To help us all pray with people in heavily indebted countries I have tried to find stories of ordinary people, ordinary neighbours, who like the people Jesus met at the bottom of the mountain, are trying to get on with ordinary lives. Through their stories I hope that we will be able to sustain our commitment to pray with each other for a whole year. This may not be an easy discipleship but it could change us all. Stories from heavily indebted countries feature again after Easter.

Janet Lees

pray for the G8 and the P8

You will need: small candles, 8 of one colour and 8 of another, and a map of the world.
Name each country aloud and light a small candle (one colour for G8 and the other for P8 countries). Put each candle on the map where the named country is shown. Look at the pattern they make. After a time of reflection move the candles around to make another pattern of your choice. Now reflect on that pattern.

Read   Joel 2.1-2,12-17

Now is the time for fasting and weeping and mourning!
Now is the time of preparation for all God's children!
Now is the time when the day of the Lord is near!

God of anticipation, help us to see with our hearts
when we strain to glimpse the clouds on which you will come,
but only notice the darkness of despair and the gloom of fear.
In blindness we weep:
When will the Lord's day be here?

God of expectation, help us to listen with our hearts
when we strain to hear the trumpets signalling your arrival,
but only detect the shouts of conflict and the cries of hunger.
In pain we cry out:
When will the Lord's day be here?

We confess with hearts broken by what we see and hear:
torn by hypocrisy as we dare to call ourselves Christ's followers;
wrenched by guilt in the midst of our own extravagant celebration;
divided by our own conflicts in the midst of a fear for change.

Let us see our hearts opened, prepared to believe.
Lord, pour your forgiving love into our hearts.
Let us hear your call: "Repent and return to me!"
Lord, we return with all our heart!

May we be trumpets, heralding your arrival:
The day of the Lord is here!
May we be clouds, writing your good news across the skies:
The day of the Lord is here!
Our forgiving God is with us!

During Lent we will be following a theme based around the person of Jesus. To begin this process of reflection in your group, or alone, try to think of as many ways you can to finish the sentence 'Jesus who.....'. For example

Jesus who ....
lived in Nazareth
knew intimately Simon Peter, Andrew, Martha and Mary
lived, died and rose again
got angry
believes in me

Put the comments on small pieces of paper and then pin them to an empty cross shape as a focus for your worship group. Conclude your activity by saying the Jesus prayer

Lord Jesus Christ,
Son of God,
be merciful to me,
a sinner.

Read   Genesis 9.8-17

Forgiving God, who listens to our empty apologies like a bruised
parent
who still washes us clean with tides of compassion,
Let us reach for the shore and rest in your shade.

Healing God, whose ears are warm to the troubles and pain of
deflated people,
we search for your promise in a place without colour.
Lead us out of the shadows and into your light.

Encircling God, who cradles heavy sorrows
when hot tears crawl from wide eyes and
hearts bleed with torn ambitions,
Guide us to the rainbow's arc, let us cuddle in your shelter.

Welcoming God, who gathers scattered people
that remain unreached by outstretched arms,
**Strengthen us to shelter others and share the hope of your
promise.**

Challenging God, who breathes with us, stops us in our paths
and unfolding comfortable routines,
**Startle us with your spectrum and make our pulse dance to the
beat of rainbow celebration.**

Jesus who... went into the desert

In the Bible, the desert is a place both of testing and encounter with God. Every mission of proclaiming and witnessing the kingdom must be prepared in the desert, where the proximity of death stirs up our will to live and makes us experience the isolation which leads us to hunger for communion.

Gustavo Gutierrez

To say that Jesus is Chief of Initiation is to recognise in him the eldest sibling who guides to perfection those who have undergone their initiation - that is, those who, with him, have started down the road to the experience of the invisible through that which is visible, to the encounter with God through the human being, to touch eternity through the symbol of the present life.
This being said, according to initiation tradition, Jesus cannot be promoted to master without having himself been subject to the initiatory experience. The Chief who presides as initiation master must himself have undergone initiation.

Anselme Sanon

pray with partner churches in Zimbabwe.

47

Read   Genesis 17.1-7, 15-16; Mark 9.2-9

To you, God of beginnings,
Abram prayed,
transformed,
to Abraham[a], father of nations:
your everlasting promise was made.

By you, God of miracles,
Sarai was blessed,
transformed,
to Sarah[s], mother of nations:
your everlasting promise was given.

From you, our father and our mother,
nations turned away,
deformed,
into people, abusive and divisive:
your everlasting promise was forgotten.

Through you, God of new life,
Jesus was reborn,
transformed,
the Son shining, brighter than brilliance:
your hidden promise was revealed.

Our mother and our father:
in you, new birth transforms our death!
Our maker and our re-shaper:
by your Spirit, you transformed Jesus!
Our teacher and our dearest companion:
your Son, Christ transformer of our lives!

---

[a] 'Abraham' sounds like the Hebrew for 'ancestor of many nations'
[s] "Sarah" in Hebrew means 'princess'

Jesus who.... suffered

Lydia Lascano, a community organizer for slum dwellers in the Philippines for more than ten years, who has presented her experience of Jesus as a suffering servant actively present with Filipino women in their suffering and resistance. She believes Jesus' suffering has two different moments. One is "passive" and the other is "active". She identifies poor Filipino women's suffering under colonialism, military dictatorship, and male domination with the passive suffering of Jesus: 'a things despised and rejected by men, a man of sorrows familiar with suffering' (Isaiah 53.3).

Lascano sees that the humiliation and dehumanisation of the suffering servant are the same as the core experience of Filipino women who are "suffering passively without hope of freeing themselves" due to the overwhelming hardship of their day-to-day survival and the unawareness of the root causes of their oppression. This is very important for poor Filipino women because they can trust Jesus for his lived suffering. Jesus does not lecture or preach about suffering in the way the institutional church does. He knows women's suffering because he was the one who once suffered helplessly like them.

Lascano also identifies an active moment of Jesus' suffering which contrasts to the passive moment. The active moment of Jesus's suffering is "doing" and "accompanying" as acts of solidarity. For her, to accompany is to be beside and walk with someone. Jesus is actively present in the Filipino women's struggle for liberation, accompanying them in their doing justice. Jesus is not a dispassionate observer of their struggle. Rather, Jesus is an active participant in their fight for justice.

For Filipino women Jesus is neither a masochist who enjoys suffering, nor a father's boy who blindly does what he is told to do. On the contrary, he is a compassionate man of integrity who identified himself with the oppressed. This image gives Asian women the wisdom to differentiate between the suffering imposed by an oppressor and the suffering that is the consequence of one's stand for justice and human dignity.

Chung Hyun Kyung

pray with partner churches in the East Asia Region of CWM.

Inspiring Change

'I am the Lord your God'

Mother
Father
Neighbour
Carer
God who nurtures and values families of all shapes,
help us to offer this love in our time shared with others.

Carpenter
Teacher
Farmer
Leader
God who explains how our world can be better and is angered
by our commercial needs, make us active in the pursuit of a fair world.

Creating
Forgiving
Healing
Sharing
God who accepts our imperfections and recognises our mistakes,
humble us that we may forgive others with greater ease.

Enduring
Ensuring
Enabling
Exciting
God who empowers our achievements, make us eager to respond
to issues that outrage us
so that we too can be passionate and persistent about building
change.

You are the Lord our God, our parent
helping us to grow and learn with your overwhelming love and
support,
encourage us to chase your example
and promote justice within local and global communities.

Jesus who.... was not always popular

A new and particularly unsettling insight for the group was the fact that *Jesus was not liked by everybody*. The general understanding amongst the group had been that Jesus was a good upright citizen who was respected by everybody for his miracles and wise teaching. However, as the group placed Jesus within his own social setting, it became apparent to them that some members of society found him particularly offensive. This 'locating' of Jesus also made him much more human and accessible to the group, and provided the opportunity for the group to voice their own (and their community's) questions about Jesus and Christianity.

Graham Philpott

'We see clearly those who did not like Jesus at the time of his trial. It was not the ordinary people who were accusing him, but rather the upper classes. These were the pharisees and elders, and even those businessmen (selling doves in the temple). The upper classes were oppressing the people, which was contradicting what Jesus was doing and teaching.'

Summary by a bible study group in Amawoti, Natal

pray with partner churches in South Africa.

God of our ancestors,
we wander through the wilderness of Lent
searching for the light which will lead us to freedom.

We gaze into our own darkness,
refusing to look at your Son on the cross, a gruesome pin-up,
as we take the opportunity to betray him once again,
Light of life, forgive us
and illuminate the darkness of our lives.

We moan selfishly
about our own self-inflicted hunger and thirst, ignoring others'
needs,
whilst we push away the plate and cup you offer:
Light of life, forgive us
and illuminate the darkness of our lives.

We can become poisoned
by our own negative outlook on the world around us,
as we continually ignore all the goodness you place there:
Light of life, forgive us
and illuminate the darkness of our lives.

We can feel abandoned
by you, your precious Son and the church,
but we still allow others to do our believing for us:
Light of life, forgive us
and illuminate the darkness of our lives.
Release us from our human ways
that we may take your light to all who search for jubilee!

Jesus who....

... is my strength. He is the one who enables and empowers me to carry on my every day work. He helps me to cope with the hardships I face daily.
...is my saviour. I live in an area where there are so many witches and evil forces that people have had to sell their property and gone in search of safer places. I believe that Jesus is a victorious Lord who conquered all evil spiritual forces and brought them under control.
...is my hope, and he gives me courage to be. He makes everything meaningful when in my everyday living I try to make my existence original and creative.
...is my saviour, my model, my helper, my teacher, my everything and my God.
...is my closest friend, who gives me light when everything about me is dark. Jesus accepts all women and men as equals; in him there is no discrimination.
...is the core of my life; he is my helper, my comforter, my refuge, and my closest friend. He teaches me to be tolerant and understanding towards the weakness of others.
Six African women answer the question 'Who is Jesus Christ in your life?'

For African women Jesus Christ is the victorious conquerer of all evil spiritual forces; he is the nurturer of life and a totality of their being. Christ is the liberator of the sufferers, the restorer of all those who are broken, the giver of hope and the courage to be. Despite the threatening hardships encountered in women's daily lives, he is the one who calls all people forth to mutually participate in the creation of a better world for all.
Anne Nasimiyu-Wasike

Who is Jesus Christ in your experience?
Which answer do you most relate to? Discuss this in a group.
Invite group members to write their answer to the question on a piece of paper and swap answers with another group member. If doing the exercise alone, post your answer back to yourself so that, later in the week, you get a reminder to think about this question again.

---

pray with partner churches in Botswana and Namibia.

Sorry

Hear my heart Lord when I am sad.
A moment when I am crowded by my own company
and my thoughts like lead weights unsettle my balance;
I am exposed.
I fill my crumpled clothes with disjointed memories and jagged
thoughts.
I force you to witness every falter, to let me see the hurt I have caused
others.
I see images of eyes flooding when my words have lashed.
I know that my diary did not share minutes with those who asked for
seconds.
It makes me cringe to see just how important the word 'I' becomes
making it easy to trample carelessly on the needs of others.
As I spill these thoughts, there are other occasions that sink my pride.
In this stillness I bring these to you.
(Silence)

With my head stooped but eyes wide open, I tiptoe into your
presence.
Quietly flicking my scrapbook collection of tainted experiences.
I have hurt you Father because you absorbed all where I have
pretended not to look.
With cupped palms, I offer to you the disappointing failures that the
mirror hides.
I know that I have done wrong, and I wear the blame awkwardly.
But I come to ask your forgiveness, for you to restore my crushed
spirit
that I may not drift into temptation,
because loving Father,
I am sorry.

Jesus who....prayed

Is it odd that Jesus, who we call God, should pray to his Father, who we call God ? Well odd or not, it says something about prayer and something about God. Prayer is so important to God, that God even does it within God's self.

Janet Lees

A man of Muslim faith walked into my office on one occasion, and asked me to pray with him. "I've just heard from Pakistan that my mother died a few minutes ago. Will you please stop and pray ?" That is just what we did. The other office staff joined us too. It was a remarkable moment in which death united people of different faiths in prayer. No-one asked the theologically vexed question: "Can we pray together as people of different faiths ?"

Inderjit Bhogal

pray with partner churches in the Netherlands and the European Region of CWM and with local people working between different faith groups.

Read   Mark 14.1 - 15. 47

A prayer for three voices

1   Manger Child, born in the night
2   Man of Sorrows, crucified in the dimness of day
3   Messiah, risen Lord of the morning

1   Wrapped in strands of cloth.
2   Stripped of purple cloaked dignity.
3   Nakedly embracing our blame.

1   Worshiped by shepherds, cherished by a mother's kiss.
2   Mocked by soldiers, whipped by men that spat your name.
3   Entrusted by God, you oozed with pain and prayed for their forgiveness.

1   'To you is born a Saviour'
2   'Hail, King of the Jews'
3   'Truly this man was God's Son'

1   Prince of Peace they named you, in awe they adored your barnlit birth
2   Crowned with thorns that pierced flesh, they shouted 'Crucify him'
3   Son of the Father, in love you showed the ultimate act of giving.

1   Gurgles eased through gaps in the timber cot.
2   Staggered cries of a dying man as nails slammed into wood.
3   A body branches on a silent cross.

1   Man of the people,
2   Alone.
3   Anticipating the Kingdom's promise.

1   The star that thinking men followed eclipsed.
2   The shadow of a wronged man covered the place where the child had lay.
3   Darkness came over the world, your fingers unclenched with the last exhausted breath.

Father God, allow us to understand how your own child's pain was for our healing.
and help us to live the hope your unconditional love inspires within us all.

Jesus who.... died

He was in his early thirties when he died. In the UK life
expectancy for males is currently 74 years and only 2.6% of the
adult population are not expected to survive to the age of 40.
The most common causes of death amongst young men will be
road accidents and even suicide. Death by violent military regime
is not a common cause here.

Around the world the story may be very different. Of the eight
poor countries mentioned during Epiphany Malawi has the lowest
life expectancy for men: 40 years, with Mozambique, Ethiopia and
Tanzania all under 50 years. In Mozambique as much as 44% of
the adult population is not expected to survive to age 40. These
figures are echoed in other neighbouring countries like Zambia and
Zimbabwe where AIDS is a common cause of death amongst
young adults.

Death by violent military regime continues to occur, often preceded
by torture. Amnesty International continues to be concerned about
this world-wide.

Christian Aid

pray with partner churches in Madagascar, and the Africa
Region of CWM.

Holy Week

For the Holy Week prayer pilgrimage here is work by Andrew Stuart, Vicki Terrell and Rebecca Latham. Andrew and Vicki who both have cerebral palsy have reflected on their experience of pilgrimage to express the week in words, whilst Rebecca's reflection is in images.

Andrew Stuart

I have been asked to write a few words about Andrew. Andrew is my son. He is a very special young man. An accident at birth caused Andrew's disability, that of Cerebral Palsy. For the first 16 years of his life, Andrew had no formal means of communication. Consequently many of his prayers focus on the gift of communication. Being a 'son of the manse', Andrew has always attended Church. We have brought him up believing that 'the chief end of man is to glorify God'. This has been the main focus of Andrew's life. During the 'silent years' we now realise that Andrew learnt the words of scripture and the words of hymns that he heard, Sunday by Sunday in Church. Those words come out strongly in his writings.

Four years ago, a wonderful breakthrough was made when a brilliant speech therapist, called Judy, painstakingly taught Andrew how to communicate using a computer called a Liberator. What a liberation experience that was. Four years later, these are Andrew's first formal writings.

How were the prayers produced? I would read the relevant passage of scripture to Andrew. He would think and then start to share his thinking so that we could focus on one particular passage at a time. Slowly he would formulate the prayer on his Liberator and I would type his words into our computer.

Andrew has no educational qualifications. His style of writing is purely and simply his own. His thoughts are often profound. Sharing those thoughts with you is a very real privilege.

Why was Andrew chosen to write for Holy Week? About five years ago, Andrew came with us on a visit to the Holy Land. This was during his silent years. It was a difficult time for him, as there was so much going on and he was unable to share his thoughts. Anyone who knows the noise and bustle of Jerusalem will know how bewildering it can be. However, that journey was a deeply moving time for Andrew as he came to terms with the nature of his disability. He visited places where Jesus walked, talked and healed many people. Now that he is able to communicate, he speaks movingly of how he perceives Jesus would have cared for him, had he been born 2000 years ago. For Andrew, there is no doubt, Jesus cares for him, every moment of his life.

Christine Stuart

Different perspective

For 30 years people have encouraged me to overcome my disability. Yet it is part of me and gives me insights and a perspective that I would not have if I didn't have cerebral palsy. I have always apologised for the inconvenience caused to other people through my disability, but it is a part of me. As I grow in self confidence I learn that my disability does not have to be a source of shame; rather it can be a gift that can be offered to others.

You call me on O Christ,
beyond the present pain;
calling from the future.
Yet you are with me now,
encouraging into paths of my day dreaming:
dreams without form,
dreams waiting to be dreamt.
You are in them,
waiting for me to awaken,
challenging the boundaries of my consciousness.
I ask for courage on the journey.

Vicki Terrell

Jesus
You must have loved Lazarus a lot
to bring him back from the dead.
You must have felt so at home
with Martha, Mary and Lazarus.
When Mary washed your feet with perfume
did it make you feel very treasured?
Did it help you prepare for your walk into Jerusalem?

The magic of the moment was broken by Judas.
You were brought back to the reality of that week.
The perfume could be sold for silver.

Dear God
You must have felt so sad
to see your son about to be betrayed
by such a close friend,
a friend chosen by Jesus himself.

Help us to travel with Jesus
to Jerusalem.
Help us in our life's journey
to face with courage
the challenges which lie ahead.
Help us to travel to our Jerusalem.

Read   **Psalm 71.1-14; John 12.20-36**

Dear God
We pray for the world

May the poor know your love.
May the blind see your truth.
Where there is darkness,
let there be light
to bring hope to all people.

Help those who are bound
by chains of
debt
illness
age
homelessness
despair
to BREAK FREE FROM THE CHAINS
that bind them
and bring them into
your light of hope.

May it be that
their hour has come.
May their darkness be banished.
May they walk in the light of Your love.

Help us in our darkest hour
to realise that You will always be with us.

Read   Isaiah 50.4-9a; Hebrews 12.1-3

Dear God

We sometimes hurt you
as much as those who surrounded you
at the time of your arrest and trial.

Our words whip and lash you
Every time we are unkind to others.

The names we call others
whip and lash you.

Spastic
Dumb
Poof
Nigger

It is you Lord who help others bear the pain
of the cruel taunt.
It is you who help those who are rejected by society.

Help us not to wound and reject others.

Help us to accept each other as we are.

Read John 13.1-17, 31b-35; 1 Corinthians 11.23-26

The Passover meal
to be shared with family and friends.
No one realised that it would be your last meal with them.
You washed their feet.
Peter objected.
He found it hard to realise what you were saying.

How often do we hear but not understand?
How often do we think that we know best?

You gave your friends a new commandment
To love one another.

Help us to love one another.
Help us to be willing to make sacrifices for others.

Every time that we break your bread
help us to share your love.

Every time that we drink your cup
help us to live your love.

Help us to welcome all to your table for
you said drink with me
ALL who are thirsty.

Holy Thursday

We all need to wash feet

From the way people often speak I get the impression that people with disabilities are to be ministered to by the church, and that 'the ministry of the disabled' are to be 'disabled', thus having a passive ministry of being ministered to. However, as a person with a living faith who happens to have a disability, I find this attitude can be a cop out, for not seeing people with disabilities primarily as people. Christ washed the disciples' feet in the Christian community. Perhaps some of us with disabilities may need some help in the actual washing of the feet but that does not mean we are exempt from the command. It might mean some good old Kiwi ingenuity in the mechanics of it!

Vicki Terrell

Read   **Psalm 22; John 18.1-19, 42**

> Dear Lord
> What a jeering mocking hell
> you met
> two thousand years ago,
> as you carried your cross
> through the streets of Jerusalem.

Would we have cheered or would we have wept on that bleak day, we call Good Friday?

Did you hold out your arms in desperation and despair - or in love, as you hung upon the cross?

What did you see, as you hung there, a sea of cheering faces, or faces torn apart with grief?

You cried out, My God, my God, why hast thou forsaken me. You know what we feel like.

> You saw your mother
> and you cared for her.
> You made time to love
> even at the time of your
> greatest pain.
> You surrounded others
> with your love
> just as you surround us
> at our worst moments
> with your love.
> Here, at the foot of your cross
> my heart is racked with pain
> until I experience the overwhelming,
> healing,
> warmth of your love.

Read   **Matthew 27.57-66; Job 14.1-14**

Holy Saturday is such a special day
Because we remember Jesus.

Less than a week ago
He was welcomed into Jerusalem
By cheering crowds.

Now he's dead.

Look at the two Marys
sitting opposite the grave.
They are so sad.
They feel helpless and powerless.

The tomb is sealed.
It is so final.

Your enemies couldn't leave you alone
even at this time.
They were afraid of you, even when you were dead.

Oh God, you are the Lord of all beings.
Comfort all who mourn
grant them your peace.

Praying with CWM Churches 2000

Please use this leaflet as a part of your prayer life, individually or corporately, within a congregation. Suggestions for prayer can be supplemented and updated by using the prayer section of CWM's journal, Inside Out, available from your church offices.

Africa

United Congregational Church of Southern Africa (UCCSA)
(comprising synods in Botswana, Mozambique, Namibia, South Africa and Zimbabwe)

Pray that:

◆ God will empower UCCSA to help deal with the HIV/AIDS crisis that is affecting southern Africa. Many children are becoming orphans because of

the virus, so please pray that they will be taken care of;

◆ UCCSA will help the poor and the unemployed in the region;

◆ The church will play an active part in continuing to heal South Africa of the wounds created by years of racism;

◆ The leaders of the region's nations will have wisdom and strength to stop fighting each other.

A women's group in Mozambique.

United Church of Zambia (UCZ)

Please thank God for the church's growth. Pray:

Soweto market, Lusaka.

◆ That the church will remain faithful to its calling and be sensitive to the needs of the communities it serves;

◆ That UCZ will raise and train enough lay and clerical workers to staff the parishes, colleges, schools and hospitals;

◆ For effective stewardship, communication and self-support.

Churches of Christ in Malawi (CCM)

Pray for:
- ◆ CCM as it sets up self-support projects which will help local communities;
- ◆ CCM as it increases the representation of women and youth at different levels in the church. They are now on the central council and are officially involved in preaching;
- ◆ The training of preachers and pastors.

Presbyterian Church of Southern Africa (PCSA)
(comprising presbyteries in South Africa, Zambia and Zimbabwe)

Give thanks for the uniting of the Presbyterian Church of Southern Africa with the Reformed Presbyterian Church of South Africa at the 1999 general assembly to form the Uniting Presbyterian Church in Southern Africa (UPCSA).

Pray for:
- ◆ The first moderator of UPCSA, Rev Clifford Leeuw;
- ◆ The restructuring of the new church's committee and general assembly office;
- ◆ The church to have a holistic ministry in southern Africa, which is experiencing change, economic problems, crime and an education crisis.

South Africa's gun culture is a major cause of crime.

Church of Jesus Christ in Madagascar (FJKM)

Please pray:
- ◆ That the churches in Madagascar may truly be witnesses to justice and peace as corruption is rife in all spheres of life in the nation;
- ◆ For all those involved in theological education with FJKM;
- ◆ For renewal within congregations and individuals, in the relationship between the Lord and his people, and in the relationships between God's people.

Pacific

Nauru Congregational Church (NCC)

Please pray:
♦ That the country will recover from the environmental damage caused by phosphate extraction;
♦ For the Christian Youth Fellowship, which is active in worship, organises bible camps and does community work such as prison, hospital and elderly visiting;
♦ For the church's involvement in preparing the curriculum for religious instruction in primary and secondary schools.

United Church in Papua New Guinea (UCPNG)

Please pray:
♦ That God will give a spirit of wisdom and understanding to foster unity within the nation's 800 different cultural groups;
♦ That the church will fight against the corrupt practices that are apparent in government and business circles;
♦ For the conservation of the country's forests. They are being cut down at an alarming rate, which is endangering marine and wildlife.

Kiribati Protestant Church (KPC)

Please pray for:
♦ The re-empowerment of youth for mission church programme, involving evangelistic outreach, local community work and leadership training;
♦ The church's ministry to inactive Christians and those who have abandoned the faith;
♦ The promotion of bible studies in village congregations to help strengthen faith and witness in rural areas.

Presbyterian Church of Aotearoa New Zealand (PCANZ)

Pray that:
♦ PCANZ congregations will enable people influenced by secularisation to respond to the Good News of Jesus Christ;
♦ The different cultures of PCANZ might have space to flourish in, so that our diversity might witness to God's creativity and oneness;
♦ The centennial of the union of the northern and southern churches to form PCANZ might be a time of thankfulness and hope.

Congregational Christian Church in American Samoa (CCCAS)

Please pray that:
◆ CCCAS churches will be well equipped for mission as they enter the next millennium;
◆ Young people will be at the heart of mission and church growth;
◆ Leadership seminars will continue to aid spiritual renewal.

Congregational Union of New Zealand (CUNZ)

Pray:
◆ For the two new churches that have joined CUNZ: the Mangere church, made up of Niueans, and Mount Wellington, made up of Samoans;
◆ For the new mission enabler;
◆ That the churches will continue to put pressure on the government to care for the marginalised and unemployed in New Zealand.

United Church in the Solomon Islands (UCSI)

Pray that:
◆ The church's strategic mission planning for the next five years will be inspired by the Holy Spirit;
◆ The church develops its pastoral ministry to meet the needs of its members;
◆ The outreach to the three new UCSI missionary areas in the Solomon Islands – Malaita, Temotu and Guadalcanal – will lead people to Christ.

Congregational Christian Church in Samoa (CCCS)

Give thanks and pray for:
◆ The financial assistance given to CCCS by overseas churches for its multipurpose youth hall, the School of Fine Arts, in Leulumoega Fou, the church schools and the theological college;
◆ The overseas mission of the CCCS and for the church's social projects among our people.

Ekalesia Kelisiano Tuvalu (EKT)

Pray for:
◆ The EKT's mission outreach as it continues its campaign to raise awareness about HIV/AIDS;
◆ The church's women's fellowship as they continue their struggle towards women's ordination;
◆ EKT's chaplaincy to merchant seamen.

East Asia

Presbyterian Church in Taiwan (PCT)

Pray for:
◆ The Reading the Bible with New Eyes campaign: to challenge our members to apply scriptural truths to their lives and to the modern world;
◆ The Neighbourhood Mission campaign: the community projects, the mass media work (medical institutions are cooperating to establish a radio network), and the prison ministry;
◆ Aborigine concerns: to promote the teaching and use of their mother tongue and ethnic culture, for the aborigine ministry in urban communities, and for aborigine employment;
◆ The Year of Youth: to present the Gospel in ways that will bring youth and students to turn to God;
◆ Justice and peace in the Asia-Pacific region: Taiwan's right to determine its own future and to work for peaceful co-existence among the nations in our area;
◆ International relations: breaking Taiwan's isolation in the international community.

Presbyterian Church in Singapore (PCS)

Please pray:
◆ That PCS will prepare effectively for the challenge of the next century by developing a vision for mission and ministry;
◆ For the partnership of global evangelism of which PCS is a part;

Boys Brigade at a PCS school.

◆ For the partnership between the English Presbytery Mission Board and the Chinese Presbytery Mission Board for local church planting and overseas mission work;
◆ For the people of Singapore hit by the financial crisis.

Presbyterian Church of Korea (PCK)

Pray:

♦ That the leaders of Korea will humbly seek God's guidance and wisdom while also heeding the needs of the people;

♦ That PCK may continue to serve the weak, the sick, the homeless, and the marginalised through ministries of mercy and love;

♦ For the people of North Korea who are undergoing famine and human rights abuses;

♦ For the peaceful reconciliation of North and South Korea;

♦ That the Holy Spirit will guide PCK missionaries working at home or abroad.

A PCK church in Seoul.

Gereja Presbyterian Malaysia (GPM)

Pray:

♦ For peace in Malaysia as it has suffered from social unrest for several years;

♦ For those affected by the economic hardships;

♦ That the church will be a beacon of light in these difficult times and that it will care for people affected by the unrest.

Hong Kong Council of the Church of Christ in China (HKCCCC)

Please pray for:

♦ The people of Hong Kong facing economic recession and hardship as the Asian financial crisis continues;

♦ HKCCCC's efforts to establish better links with the Chinese churches on national and local levels;

♦ Better cooperation between HKCCCC congregations and the church's primary and secondary schools to enhance evangelical action among students;

♦ The church's work as it witnesses God's Word and calls people to him.

Europe

Reformed Churches in the Netherlands (RCN)

The decline in membership of the mainline churches in the Netherlands is slowing and there are increasing contacts with Evangelicals, Pentecostals and Charismatics. Pray that these talks will lead to greater cooperation.

Pray for:
◆ The Reformed Churches in the Netherlands and the Evangelical Lutheran Church in the Kingdom, which officially united on 1st December 1999 to form the Netherlands Reformed Church;
◆ RCN's cooperation with immigrant churches.

Union of Welsh Independents (UWI)

Give thanks for:
◆ The many churches with committed people working and praying for renewal and that have responded to the call to be more involved in mission in their communities and worldwide;
◆ The appointment of the UWI's new general secretary.

Pray:
◆ That God will breathe new spiritual life into the UWI and into Wales to counter the fall in church-going;
◆ For more candidates for Christian ministry;
◆ That churches will find new ways of doing mission in Wales;
◆ For the new UWI general secretary, Dewi Myrddin Hughes.

Presbyterian Church of Wales (PCW)

Give thanks for:
◆ The continuing growth and success of PCW's outreach among children and young people and the leadership provided by the church's team of dedicated workers;
◆ The ever closer relationships between the churches in Wales.

Pray for:
◆ The success of the dialogue to form an United Free Church and to find agreement to appoint an ecumenical bishop.

Congregational Federation (CF)

Give thanks for the increase in membership of many of the CF's churches and for the Christian literature ministry at the CF's headquarters in Nottingham.

Pray for:
◆ The ongoing development of CF's mission programme: two regional training coordinators seek to equip people for ministry and mission and a growing network of area mission enablers helps congregations assess their mission context;
◆ The recruitment of ministers, as this is increasingly difficult;
◆ The renewal of the Holy Spirit in each CF church as women, men and children acknowledge their vital role in the local community.

Congregational Union of Scotland (CUS)

Give thanks for the caring, healing and reconciling work done by voluntary organisations in Scotland.

Pray:
◆ That the people of Scotland find in their new Parliament a fuller expression of their national and international aspirations and obligations;
◆ For the unity of the Church in Scotland so that it may tell and live out the Gospel of Jesus Christ with faithfulness, creativity, adventurousness and determination.

United Reformed Church
in the United Kingdom (URCUK)

Give thanks for:
◆ The generosity of church members through the ages, providing the funds enabling the church to make new investments in mission today;
◆ New developments in the church's life and witness locally, regionally and nationally.

Please pray:
◆ For the URCUK as it continues to wrestle with divisive but important issues around human sexuality;
◆ That the URCUK may discover a fresh sense of purpose as a partner in God's mission in the UK today;
◆ That the union with the Congregational Union of Scotland may proceed smoothly, and that it will enrich the life and witness of both churches.

South Asia

Presbyterian Church of India (PCI)

Please pray:

◆ That God will bless PCI's leadership with wisdom and strength to lead the church through India's changing socio-political situation;

◆ That PCI's journey into the new millennium will be with renewed faith;

◆ For Indian Christians who are facing acute poverty and suffering owing to natural disasters and displacement because of ethnic conflicts;

◆ That the young people in India who are searching for meaning in life may find Jesus.

Women from PCI.

Church of South India (CSI)

Please pray:

◆ That Indians learn to trust each other. Hindu fundamentalists have increased their attacks on minority groups, and on Christians in particular;

Vacation bible school, Hudson Memorial Church, Bangalore.

◆ That Christians will show love and compassion to other people as an expression of the love of Christ;

◆ For the church as it continues its struggle against injustice and oppressive social structures. In particular, it tries to help the poor, women and children.

Church of Bangladesh (CoB)

Please pray:
- ◆ For the church's Social Development Project. This provides health care, literacy training, runs primary and secondary schools and empowers women;
- ◆ That this project will be an effective way of witnessing the Christian faith as many of those on this programme are non-Christians;
- ◆ For the poor people in Bangladesh, for those affected by disease and hunger, and for the many victims of road accidents.

Front cover: A Bangladeshi liturgical dance.

Church of North India (CNI)

Pray for plans to:
- ◆ Identify training needs and resource people at synod and regional levels;
- ◆ Offer training in communication, community organisation, leadership development, human rights, legal aid, outreach and community health;
- ◆ Upgrade facilities at regional and diocesan levels;
- ◆ Organise workshops to revive Sunday schools, women's fellowships and youth programmes.

Pray also for CNI's commitment to unity, mission and evangelism, leadership development, solidarity with the marginalised, inter-faith dialogue, the indigenisation of worship and more democratic use of power in the church.

A CWM *regional communication training workshop*.

Presbyterian Church of Myanmar (PCM)

Pray:
- ◆ For the baby home for abandoned children run by the church;
- ◆ That the church's mission outreach will bring people to Christ;
- ◆ That PCM's theological education will help ministers in their work for God.

Caribbean

United Church in Jamaica and the Cayman Islands (UCJCI)

Pray:

◆ That UCJCI will respond effectively to the fall in moral values and the rise in violence in society;

◆ That the church will meet the needs of the increasingly jobless youth, disabled people and the growing number of elderly;

◆ For visionary leadership to move the church from maintenance to mission.

A school for the deaf in Kingston.

Guyana Congregational Union (GCU)

Pray for:

◆ The church to develop a clear vision for the way ahead;

◆ The easing of economic tension affecting the country, and its social consequences, and for genuine cooperation, unity and peace within Guyana;

Children from GCU.

◆ The new lay pastors who graduated from the lay pastors' training programme, and that their knowledge, zeal and enthusiasm will have an impact on local congregations.

Council for World Mission, Ipalo House, 32-34 Great Peter Street, London SW1P 2DB, UK
Tel: +44 (0)20 7222 4214   Fax: +44 (0)20 7233 1747 or +44 (0)20 7222 3510
Email: council@cwmission.org.uk   http://www.cwmission.org.uk   Registered Charity No 232868
Printed by Healeys Printers, Ipswich, UK

We wait. Christ needs us
at this dark lonely hour
in agony of knowledge.
He needs us
to be with him,
just as we need each other
in the dark lonely hours,
in our agonies.

Vicki Terrell

Read **John 20.1-18**

With a heavy heart Mary went to your tomb.
Would the guards help her roll away the stone?

The stone has gone!
God, what has happened to the body?

Mary did not understand,
she wept.
She went into the garden
and met you.
She did not recognise you
until you spoke one word,
her name —-Mary.

Mary was overjoyed.

Jesus is alive.

Help us to recognise you,
each time you call us by name.
Help us to be overjoyed
and to know that you are alive
forever more.

Alleluia!
Christ is risen.
Alleluia!

Enabling and disabling each other

I am aware of people enabling or disabling me through attitudes towards disability. At times people have encouraged me to do something I had though impossible and I have succeeded. These people enable me to grow because of their support and challenge. Other times I have been limited by other people's attitudes. When we disable each other we tend to have the attitude that we know what's best for them!

The tomb of our agony,
broken open;
empty.
Hurt is transformed:
challenged to live,
find life,
new hope.
Christ is with us,
walking with us
in new life.

Vicki Terrell

Read　　1 John 1.1-2.2

Eternal God, we know the power of human language to deceive.
When our rationalisations sound hollow and glib to us,
when we speak to edit the truth or to manipulate people,
and when what we say means more to us than what we are,

help us to recognise the Word of life.

Uniting God, ours is not the brightest chapter in your church's history,
and living the truth is still more a goal than an achievement.
When we are headstrong, self-centred, frightened and defensive,
hold us in community with you and with each other;

help us to recognise the Word of life.

Living God, as we remember the life generously given on the cross,
help us to accept the new life opened up on that first Easter.
As the light of Easter transforms our darkness,
and as we come alive each day to the depth and truth and wonder,

**enable us to see, to hear and to declare
the Word of life made flesh for humankind.**

Acts 4.32-35
Psalm 133   1 John 1.1-2.2
John 20.19-31

Easter 2

The Tabora beekeepers live in a remote part of western Tanzania, on the edge of the tropical forest. Their co-operative was formed in 1962 and is the longest surviving co-op in Tanzania. Membership of the co-operative is open to all families within the community, and it is run democratically by an elected board. The co-op owns two trucks for collecting the honey from the forest and a factory for processing it and storing it.

But the co-op is about more than just honey production. They have been involved in a number of community projects such as primary schools and a clinic, and have developed some money-making projects for themselves, such as a shop and a maize meal plant where members can take their maize to be ground. As well as making money for the co-op, these serve the community and save the expense of travelling and paying higher prices elsewhere.

Shared Interest

Tanzania received £6,300 worth of pound coins sent to the Treasury by people responding to the Christian Aid debt relief campaign. The coins were taped to postcards urging the Chancellor, Gordon Brown, to cancel Third World debt. He decided that the money should go towards wiping out Tanzania's debt of $7.4 million.

News item from April 1998

75

Living risen Christ, open our minds to understand the scriptures.

The disciples' healing miracles make us uneasy.
Should we feel like failures when we are scared to try?
Is physical healing a real gauge of faith or are we missing the point?

Living risen Christ, open our minds to understand the scriptures.

The psalmist sounds quite self-righteous in number 4.
If we spoke like that, people would call us smug and proud.
Have we a special relationship? Is it OK to be proud?

Living risen Christ, open our minds to understand the scriptures.

When you took away our sins we quickly reinstated them.
Because we are not sin-free, and we don't excel at righteousness,
does it really mean we have neither seen you nor known you?

Living risen Christ, open our minds to understand the scriptures.

Must we think about the resurrection appearances and
                                                disappearances,
with mortal wounds in a tangible body, but eating fish?
If faith looks like naive gullibility are we getting things wrong?

Living risen Christ, open our minds to understand the scriptures.

Too often we interpret you in the light of our understanding of
                                                scriptures.
Help us to interpret the scriptures in the light of your living presence.
Help us to know you participating in our lives, in our stories.

**Living risen Christ, if faith grows in us, if we find confidence and
know forgiveness,
let it be because you are opening our minds to understand the
scriptures.**

Footprints on the Emmaus Road

Read   **Luke 24.13-35**

```
foot    tra-
prints  vel   the
in the  on   jour-
 sand        ney   from
                       birth
   Life, transient          to
  like the  impression     death
  of footprints on  a beach
 swept away by the rising tide
 the journey smooth in places
 painfully rocky  in  others
   a journey  from  birth to
    death.  Emmaus  foot-
      prints  heavy  at
       first    then
      scuffed, hurried
      running,  dancing
       the  road  from
       death to  life.
      The cross becomes
     resurrection  as
     humanity    skips
      hand  in  hand
       with God.
```

pray with partners in American Samoa, who have a door to
door visiting scheme (see CWM leaflet), and Samoa.

Read   John 10.11 - 16

What would you be today, Lord?
Still the good shepherd?
Or perhaps the fireman, the lifeboat crew member,
        the mountain rescuer, the anonymous hero?
Lord, in our age of change,
We thank you for your unfaltering love.

How would you lay down your life?
Still on the cross?
Or perhaps by the firing squad, the land mine,
        the terrorist's bomb, the electric chair?
Lord, in our age of conflict,
We thank you for your unfaltering love.

Have 2000 years changed your love?
Your love for those outside the fold?
Perhaps the rapist, the murderer,
        the paedophile, the stalker?
Lord, in our age of uncertainty,
We thank you for your unfaltering love.

Have 2000 years changed our foe?
Is it still the wolf?
Or perhaps the internet, the changing climate,
        the aggressor state, the media?
Lord, in our age of fear,
We thank you for your unfaltering love.

In Zambia most people will know someone who is ill or has died from AIDS. And they will know people who are looking after the children of a relative who has died.

The paediatric nutrition ward at Kitwe Central Hospital contains 20 cots. It is a small sunny ward painted blue and decorated with Disney characters. Babies and children under five come here when they are severely malnourished. Many of the babies are HIV positive, infected by their mothers during birth or breast feeding. The ward is eerily silent, children lying still, watched over by anxious mothers. Four out of ten children admitted to the ward will die.

The Out of School Youth Group makes and sells beds, wardrobes and kitchen chairs, as well as educating its teenage members about preventing HIV infection. They have discovered a growing market in coffins and now make them to order: as many children's coffins as adults are needed.

Violet Mwinuka is 42 years old, a widow and mother of 8 children and works as a volunteer in the Home Care Programme set up by the Ndola Catholic Diocese. She says: 'My biggest joy comes when, through my consistent care, a person feels much better and is even able to carry out some daily tasks. I am ready to face and fight the terrible AIDS and challenge the community to do the same. Doing this work has brought to the surface a total knowledge of myself and my role within the community'.

Christian Aid

Look AIDS.

I am an orphan.

I have no father.

I have no mother.

I have no aunt or uncle.

AIDS you have left me in misery.

AIDS you are cruel.

Shame.

Trudy Mukosha, aged 9 Chongwe Primary School Anti-AIDS Club

In Zambia
- 700,000 men and women are HIV positive, 8% of the population
- 600,000 children are AIDS orphans
- international debt is over \$7 billion; three times as much is spent on debt as on health services

AIDS a Living Issue, Christian Aid

pray with partner churches in Zambia, and HIV/AIDS care and prevention.

Living God, you are the vine.
So much more than the vine;
you are our sun, rain and earth.
> **Thank you for giving life.**

Living God, we are the branches.
So much less than the vine;
drawing on your strength, your power, your glory.
> **Thank you for giving life.**

Help us to live in your image;
Help us bear the fruit of your justice, peace and mercy;
where love has been long forgotten,
where anger and hatred have grown,
where pain and suffering dwell.
> **Help us bring your life.**

In different parts of the world there are people who serve God and who pray for the whole world. We might not know them directly but we want them to pray for us.

Ethiopian priest

Ethiopia has a population of 60,148,000 people who each have a life expectancy of 49 years. Each woman has an average of 7 children and one woman in 9 will die in childbirth. Only 4% of women aged 15-49 use contraception. With 93% of births taking place in the home a lack of trained birth attendants is a major factor in maternal deaths. Rather than providing a few high cost clinics a community based approach is needed. People known and trusted in their local communities are provided with low cost basic training and act as family-planning advisors making birth significantly safer for both women and their babies.

Marie Stopes International

pray with partner churches in Ethiopia, and those working on women's health projects.

Lord, God,
I don't know why you have chosen me
to be your friend.
I'm no saint !
Yet you want me,
with all my life experience
to love others,
without exception,
as you have loved me.

     Help me I pray,
     especially when I am tempted
     by the negative presumptions of my breeding,
     by the prejudice I have been taught,
     by my natural desire to pass by evil quietly
     and not to disturb it,
     to pretend I have not seen,
               nor heard suffering.

You have raised me up
from service to friendship.
You clasp my hand and make me welcome in the house of God.

I do want to serve you and do what is right.
Take me and make me worthy of such trust,
so that those who meet me
may find you;
     your love rejoicing in all I do,
     your joy dancing through my faith,
     your life offered again through my friendship.

Mozambique today is something of a success story. Nearly six million people have been successfully reintegrated into the society since the war and its economy is starting to pick up. But it still has a long way to go. In the UN ranking of countries from 1-172, in which each country is ranked according to life expectancy, education and income from 1-172 (the poorest), Mozambique still ranks as 166. There are glaring lifestyle discrepancies, especially in cities like the capital, Maputo. 'To be rich in the capital for most people means having one meal on the table per day', says one worker 'but the truly rich ride around in Mercedes. One Mercedes could pay the salaries of 25 people for 25 years'.

The Christian Council of Mozambique was instrumental in bringing peace and now they are turning peace into reconciliation and development. The priorities are water, health, education, the opening of roads, training people for employment and starting small scale projects to generate a living.

CWM 'Inside Out'

pray with partner churches in the African region of CWM.

Time to get ready

Suddenly the teacher is gone
and the pupils must learn to put his teachings into practice.
Christ has returned to the Father;
Jesus, the son of man, is glorified in the heavens,
and we must get ready
for his Spirit is to come upon us.

Lord, Fill us with the joy of the disciples coming down from the mountain;

> share with us the glory of the ascended Christ
> and prepare us to receive the gift of the Holy Spirit
> so that we may be your witnesses of salvation.

We would be your people of faith and love;
teach us the wisdom that reveals your justice and peace;
open our minds to see and to show the light of your forgiveness;
inspire us to rejoice in the hope to which you call your children;
give us a sense of the great richness of the life you promise,
and bless us with your wonderful power,

> the power that raised Christ from death,
> and seats him at God's side in heaven
> from where he rules over all nations
> all time and all creation.

Lord, Fill us with the joy of the disciples coming down from the mountain;

> share with us the glory of the ascended Christ
> and prepare us to receive the gift of the Holy Spirit
> so that we may be your witnesses of salvation.

Getting away from it all ?

Maccaroy Brown, aged 11 years, of St James URC, Sheffield, spent three months in Jamaica in early 1999. He said:
'It was all so good; climbing coconut trees, running in bare feet and swimming in the sea. The big waves would really knock you off your feet. The food was nice; yams, salt fish, akee, green bananas and cho-cho. They didn't have toilets and you had to drink rainwater. I'd like to go back there; it was warm and I liked the swimming.'

Elis Nevitt and friends set up a stall to raise awareness about Jamaica's debt at the Cricket World Cup warm-up match between Goucestershire and the West Indies at the beginning of Christian Aid Week 1999, after a visit to Jamaica earlier in the year. He said:
'This event will provide a great opportunity to bring attention to the issue of unpayable debt, and its enslaving impact on the West Indies. We hope to make people aware that things must change in order that the West Indies is included in the world economy, and not unfairly and unjustly 'declared out'.'

Christian Aid News

pray with partner churches in the Caribbean Region of CWM.

Read   John 17.6-19

As you waited,
knowing the trial to come,
you prayed for us.
And now we wait.

As you waited,
having nearly completed your task,
you prayed for us.
And now we wait.

As you waited,
still to return to the Father,
you prayed for us.
And now we wait.

As you waited,
not belonging to our world,
you prayed for us.
And now we wait.

We wait upon your life-giving Spirit.

[SILENCE]

Come, imminent breath of life, come.

[SILENCE]

The Jute Works is a co-operative marketing organisation which sells the jute craft products of over 6,000 women from all over Bangladesh, mostly in village based co-operatives. Most of the women belong to poor families with little or no land, and some of them are single, widowed or divorced. Making crafts has been their only way of making a living.

Unfortunately the demand for jute is declining, so the Jute Works has been helping the women to find additional ways of earning money, such as rearing calves or goats, or buying land to grow rice. Training and education are an important feature of the Jute Works' activities. They have helped with everything from training in making crafts and managing co-ops, to health and sanitation.

Firoza belongs to a village group making crafts. She says: 'Since becoming a member I have been able to buy enough land for us to be able to grow rice for our family'.

Shared Interest

pray with partner churches in the South Asia region of CWM.

Let your Spirit burn on

Let your Spirit burn on through the ages:
    burn down the barriers that prevent you filling our hearts;
    burn down the obstacles we place in your way.

Let the eternity of your Spirit fill this place:
    fill us as we wait for you;
    fill us for we are ready.

Let two thousand years of Christ's love enfold us:
    enfold us as a parent to a child;
    enfold us in your agape arms.

Let your Spirit burn on:
    burn away all that harms us;
    burn us so that we may be rejuvenated in you.

'If it wasn't for Prodeco-op we wouldn't have been able to afford food at all this year. The peas and beans we grow to eat were ruined by slugs so now we have to buy food. The good price we got for our coffee meant that we could afford to buy food for ourselves and our children, rather than go hungry.'

Juanita Martinez Reyes, coffee grower

Coffee Time

Make yourself or your friend a cup of fairly traded coffee and think about this ....

Challenging Spirit, as your refreshing breath
freshly warms each of us, help us to see
our God is no wheeler-dealer,
faceless financier or greedy multinational.
Sponsor us to challenge the markets of misery,
where the world is divided between
those who have coffee breaks
and those who are broken by them.
May we never be satisfied
with the warm coffee-time feeling
but struggle on together
to share the fruits of your commonwealth
with unending hope.

Janet Lees

pray for local Traidcraft representatives.

You speak to us

Read   **Isaiah 6.1-8; Psalm 29; Romans 8.12-17; John 3.1-17**

Creator God, you speak to us
as sons and daughters
and heirs of the kingdom
in sounds which reflect and resonate
signs of your greatness and glory over all creation.
Touch our lips and let us speak your words of praise
that we may cry out:
Holy, holy, holy is the Lord of Hosts:
the whole earth is full of the glory of God.

Challenging Christ, you speak to us
as sons and daughters
and heirs of the kingdom
in words which chastise and call for change
when our human speech falters and fumbles.
Touch our lips and let us speak your words of wisdom
that we may cry out:
Holy, holy, holy is the Lord of Hosts:
the whole earth is full of the glory of God.

Commissioning Spirit, you speak to us
as sons and daughters
and heirs of the kingdom
in affirmations which confirm and give confidence
to the eager expectations and hope of humankind.
Touch our lips and let us speak your words of life
that we may cry out:
Holy, holy, holy is the Lord of Hosts:
the whole earth is full of the glory of God.

In parts of Bolivia in the high Andes mountain it can be very dry. Periods without rainfall, though common enough in this, one of the poorest parts of the country, can intensify through drought conditions, especially during 'El Nino', a disturbance of the world's climate which occurs about every seven years.

The traditional way of working is co-operative, the whole community working together on each others' pieces of land; so here with advice form the Centre for Educational Advance and Research (CIPE), and tools loaned by them, a joint effort is underway to make a substantial trench so as to conserve the rainwater when it comes. From the deep trenches the water can then seep under the surface and run down the slope to water the seeds - an easier form of irrigation than carrying water from a river, and more reliable than a large number of irrigation channels. In such a way people can become more self supporting without abandoning their traditional working methods.

Christian Aid

pray with partner churches involved in irrigation and agricultural work, and for the work of CIPE in Bolivia.

You are the rock of ages,
rough hewn in our minds,
yet smoothed by time.
Your flinty presence
a stone in the eye of the oppressor,
a spark of light in our darkness.

You are the flame of passion,
still smouldering in doubtful hearts,
waiting for that gentle draught
to reignite excited zeal;
yet blazing bright
in tongues of proclamation.

You are the waters of life,
rising up to drown indifference
and break the muggy tension of injustice
with storms of fury;
your dew on the mountains
the memory of a kiss on the cheek.

You are the air of calm,
the still silence of an Alpine summit,
cold to the lungs,
yet warming the heart.
You breath life into stagnant solitude,
clearing clouds and cobwebs,
making all things new.

Earth, water, fire.

When using this prayer in worship have ready a clump of earth, a jug of water to pour into a bowl and a candle to light. Introduce these symbols before the prayer, perhaps during the singing of a hymn about God in Creation.

pray with partner churches in Papua New Guinea, and projects to conserve the country's natural resources (see CWM leaflet).

Love outside

Rainbow God
whose end extends beyond our reach,
so many feel excluded from the church.
Lead us outside,
to those who do not feel able to come in
that we may learn from their experience.

Lead us to those whose wheels of mobility
shame our narrowness,
giving us access to their experience and faith.

Lead us to those whose playful love
surpasses the limits of convention,
and let us adorn them with crimson luxury.

Lead us to those whose lonely agony of miscarried hope
has destroyed their faith in your love,
and give us the grace to sit together in silent solidarity.

Lead us to those whose youthful vigour and challenge
has been abused by unyielding tradition
and turn us to face the future.

The Jaipur Limb has been developed over the last 20 by Dr P K Sethi, an orthopaedic surgeon in Jaipur, India. He noticed that more and more of the amputees he treated were discarding their artificial limbs and reverting to crutches. He found that limbs based on western designs were proving unsuitable to the needs of the mostly rural population and set about designing and limb which would suit those needs. His ideas were brilliantly translated by local craftsmen and after many trial, the Jaipur foot was born. The Jaipur Limb can also be worn by shoe wearing urban amputees, and is now used by over a hundred thousand people in many developing countries, including new projects in Mozambique and Angola.

Facts about disability in India
- only 5% of children with disabilities go to school
- only 0.1% of people with disabilities have jobs in government institutions (the law requires 3%)
- 80% of rehabilitation facilities are in the cities and towns
- 78% of people with disabilities live in rural areas
- 50% of the population of 960 million live below the poverty line.

pray with partner churches in north India.

The Jaipur Limb Campaign is at jaipurlimb@ndirect.co.uk

Read   2 Samuel 5.1-5, 9-10; Mark 6.1-13

Youthful King,
as you anointed David, as a young man,
to reign over all Israel,
we give you thanks
for trusting a nation to the vision of a youth.

Help us to see your kingdom through the eyes of the young.

As you called Samuel, as a boy,
to speak your words of prophesy,
we ask for your openness,
that we might listen to the words of children.

Help us to see your kingdom through the eyes of the young.

As Mary sat at the feet of Jesus,
eager to learn of your life and your love,
teach us to worship you
with the devotion and imagination of children.

Help us to see your kingdom through the eyes of the young.

As Jesus, son of Mary,
shocked the leaders of the synagogue with his youthful wisdom,
challenge us
to seek out the young prophets in our congregation.

Help us to see your kingdom through the eyes of the young.

How God made the world?
    God made the world with butterflies
    and elephants going trump, trump, trump!
How God made the world ?
    God made the world with dinosaurs
    such as Tyrannosaurus Rex.
How God made the world ?
    I think that it is very good,
    in fact it is brilliant.

Hannah Warwicker, aged 5 years

What have we done, how can we mend it?
Why are we killing birds, animals, plants, trees and rivers?
Look into the future. What do you see?
Look into the past. How many differences can you find?
When you listen to the past, what do you hear?
When you listen in the future, what will you hear?
Will you notice any differences? If yes, how many?
I cannot count. I think there are too many!

Katrina Maclean, aged 11 years

 pray with partner churches in Nauru.

97

O Praise the Lord!
The world is his.
Let's move with graceful dancing feet.
We'll race the clouds
and greet the trees
and step in time to earth's heartbeat.

Exult the King!
The ark is his:
the symbol of our unity.
With tambourines
and castanets
we'll sing a song of harmony.

We turn to God
with sorry hearts
when rhythms sadly out of sync'
poison the soil,
pollute the air
and fill the seas with oily slick.

Rejoice in hope!
For life resists
the dissonance of nature's death.
She skips to cleanse,
restore, renew,
its height and depth, its length and breadth.

O Praise the Lord!
The world is his.
Let's move with graceful dancing feet.
We'll race the clouds
and greet the trees
and step in time to earth's heartbeat.

*Clearly this could be sung to any LM (8888) meter: Rockingham,
Winchester New, Solemnis haec festivitas,
or Veni Immanuel with a refrain as follows:*
> *Rejoice! Rejoice!*
> *Let's dance and sing a song of praise to our Creator King.*

This artwork for this week was inspired by a drawing by Wil Muk'willixw (Art Wilson), a First Nations Artist from the Canadian West Coast.

We affirm that what unites us is stronger than what separates us; neither failures or uncertainties, neither fear or threats will weaken our intention to continue to walk together on the way to unity; welcoming those who would join us on this journey, widening our common vision, discovering new ways of witnessing and acting together in faith.

World Council of Churches Assembly, Harare

pray with partners in Taiwan, especially those working with Aborigine concerns (see CWM leaflet), and Hong Kong.

Shepherding God,
> standing in solidarity on the harsh edge of existence,
> huddling with refugees, fending off the cold,
> struggling alongside families who barely eke out a living;

Enable us to be shepherds of justice and righteousness.

Shepherding God,
> dazzled by the opulence of our purpose-built shopping arcades,
> saddened by the incessant activity of our self-important lifestyles,
> angered by the deception of wealth and our opium of security;

Challenge us to be shepherds of justice and righteousness.

Shepherding God,
> alongside those trapped in the valley of depression and despair,
> grieving with the bereaved in their isolation and disorientation,
> sharing the dull ache that marks the loss of hope;

Entrust us to be shepherds of justice and righteousness.

Shepherding God,
> fending off the wolf pack of cruel dictators,
> standing firm against the lure and seduction of the money
> lenders,
> opposing injustice, oppression and violence in all their guises;

**Empower us to be shepherds of justice and righteousness
that all may dwell together in the house of God.**

 If possible enlarge this on a photocopier or make an overhead projector transparency and use it as a focal point whilst the prayer is being read.

 pray with partner churches in Aotearoa New Zealand.

101

Read   John 6.1-21

Invitation to Communion
Read 2 Kings 4.42-44; John 6.1-21

As Elisha received the offering of the first fruits,
and distributed them amongst those in need,
so we are reminded to give to others out of our wealth.

As a boy's mother packed a lunch of barley loaves and fish,
a lunch offered for the feeding of the multitudes,
so we are called to offer ourselves for the growing of God's kingdom.

As Mary at the wedding at Cana in Galilee,
pleads with her son to remember the outcasts served last,
so we are challenged to turn our world's priorities upside down.

As the disciples gathered to celebrate the Passover meal,
received the offering of broken bread and poured out wine,
so we too are invited to share in remembrance of that Last Supper.

So come to this table remembering the brokenness of our world,
Come to this table to celebrate the fruits of the earth,
Come to this table to be challenged and changed,

Come, it is Christ who meets us here in bread broken and wine poured.

Blessing
Read 2 Kings 4.42-44; John 6.1-21

May the blessing of the God who gives us bread,
The blessing of the Son who breaks the bread,
And the blessing of the Holy Spirit
who challenges us to share bread with the world,
Be with us all.

2 Kings 4.42-44
Psalm 145.10-18
John 6.1-21   Ephesians 3.14-21

7 after Pentecost

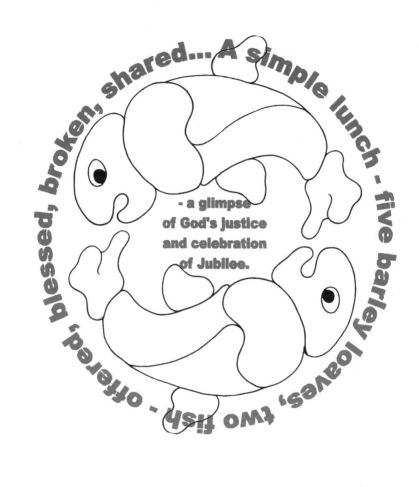

shared... A simple lunch - five barley loaves, two fish - offered, blessed, broken,

- a glimpse of God's justice and celebration of Jubilee.

prayer with partner churches in the Solomon Islands and Tuvalu.

103

Read　　**Psalm 78.23-29; John 6.24-35**

Bread of heaven,
manna raining from the skies,
the food of angels,
sustaining God's people
on their journey.

**We give you thanks
for the bread of heaven
and the fruit of the vine,
the gifts of God
for the people of God.**

Five barley loaves,
blessed, broken and shared,
the food of the earth,
soil tilled, seeds tended,
harvested in abundance.

We give you thanks...

Grapes crushed and fermented,
wine poured out,
the fruits of the earth
symbol of violent death
and sign of new life.

We give you thanks...

Many grains, many grapes,
Bread broken and wine poured,
food of earth and heaven,
gathering and uniting us
as Christ's body in God's world.

We give you thanks...

Lemise Jean-Philippe is a breadmaker who lives in Haiti. Here's her typical day.

'At about 5 in the morning, just as it is beginning to get light, I get up. I collect flour, salt, yeast, kindling wood and water. I have to take them to the bakery, which takes several journeys. I pay the foreman in advance and leave the bakers to transform my ingredients into dough. I go home and see my son off to school.

Then I set to making peanut butter. I like to make enough to last several weeks. But often, before I finish, I must leave the house again: at the bakery the dough will be ready and I must shape it into small loaves. Then its into the oven with it, and I've time to finish my cooking.

I also do what housework I can and then it's off to the bakery once more, taking my large wicker basket with me to collect the finished bread.

The smell of freshly-baked bread is wonderfully appetising, but I've no time to eat right now. Better that I take it into town to sell from my stall. I sell the bread on its own, or with peanut butter to those who feel able to treat themselves.

In a quiet moment I realise how hungry I've become, so I eat a little of my stock as I go along. It's late in the evening by the time I get home. I've lots of bread left over, so I'll be able to sell all day tomorrow.'

Christian Aid News

Sharing the Story

If you want to use this story during a communion service you need one person to read it in stages during the service. Read it as follows

- the first paragraph at the beginning as the call to worship, assembling the ingredients Lemise uses on the communion table,
- the next 2 paragraphs around the other Bible reading you will use in the service,
- the third paragraph before the communion part of the service, as the invitation to communion,
- the fourth paragraph at the moment when the bread is shared,
- the last paragraph after the communion is finished, before the close of the service.

Fleeing God,
> you fled with Elijah to the desolation of the wilderness,
> you flee today with refugees, displaced and afraid,
> with exiles driven from their homes and their land.

God of the barren place, grant your rest and protection.

Isolated God,
> you experienced the gnawing pain of Elijah's loneliness,
> you reside today in the isolation and dependency of the
> > housebound,
> with the home-sick teenager away from family for the first time.

God of the lonely, touch us with the voice of an angel.

Despairing God,
> despairing with Elijah, 'I've had enough',
> you stand with all those in the dole queues of redundancy,
> sitting in solidarity in the pits of depression and helplessness.

God of the despairing, warm us with the glimmering glow of hope.

Journeying God,
> hungry and tired, walking with Elijah as he travelled to Horeb,
> you journey with us in the pain of broken relationships,
> walking step by step through bereavement and separation.

God of the broken and weary, sustain us on life's journey.

Searching God,
> listening for a voice amidst wind, earthquake and fire,
> you are with us in the confusing storms of life,
> you are present in the sounds of sheer silence.

God of the hungry, grant us the bread of life.

1 Kings 19.4-8
Psalm 34.1-8   John 6.35, 41-51 9 after Pentecost
Ephesians 4.25-5.2

Cityscape

From old newspapers, cut out some shapes to represent buildings of different kinds and style, and stick these on a larger background piece of card to make a city landscape. This could make a temporary 'altar front' or 'table cover' for today's worship.

pray with partner churches in Korea, especially projects with homeless people (see CWM leaflet).

Call to Worship - Wisdom calls

> *Read* **Proverbs 9.1-6 (see also Proverbs 8)**

It is suggested that Voice 1 and 2 could be read from different locations in the church eg voice 1 could be read from a gallery or pulpit and voice 2 could be read from the back or side of the church. It could also be read whilst moving from the back or sides of the church towards the front ending with the final stanza being read from the front.

**Wisdom has built her house,
she has hewn her seven pillars,
and set her table before us.**

Voice 1   Wisdom calls,
calls from the highest places,
from the rugged, age old mountains,
from the hill tops and moor-lands.

Voice 2   Wisdom searches,
searches to the ends of the earth,
from the vast fathoms of the ocean deep,
to the farthest glimmers of distant galaxies.

Voice 1   Wisdom seeks,
seeks out those who desire understanding,
who value wisdom more than the richest jewels,
knowledge more than choicest gold.

Voice 2   So come, listen for the whisper of wisdom,
for the voice of insight and understanding.
Come gather at her table and share of her fruits,
of bread and wine, the offerings of earth.

**We come responding to wisdom's call,
to dwell in her house and feast at her table.**

Where is Wisdom ?

Is it wise to:
- spend less and less on health care,
- charge school fees for the poorest people,
- cause unemployment to rise to over 20% of the working population,
- replace food crops with cash crops.

These things have been happening in the world's poorest countries since the 1980s because of unpayable debt.

A woman brought her two children to a Zambian doctor. One was three years old, the other thirteen. Both were very sick. The doctor prescribed treatment. She thanked him and left. But when he saw her again some time later and asked how the children were, she told him that the younger one had died. She explained that she had not had enough money to pay for the treatment for both children, so with much pain she decided to pay for the older child's medicine. He got better quickly, but the mother had to watch her youngest child die.

Use this story as the basis for a discussion and role play. think about how the mother felt as she went to the doctor, and as she came away. Imagine what she might have said to her children, and the struggles she must have had with herself before coming to her decision. How would you feel in this situation.

Debt is tearing down schools, clinics and hospitals and the effects are no less devastating than war.

Dr Adabayo Adedeji, Nigeria

pray for the Jubilee 2000 campaign around the world.

Read Ephesians 6.10-20

As this is a rewriting of Ephesians 6.10-20 using the metaphor of Textiles rather than the metaphor of armour, it is suggested that the two are read alongside each other. This meditation could also be read by two or more voices to add variety and different fabrics could be used as part of a display.

Clothe yourselves with God's rich tapestry of textures,

Drape yourselves with the costly silk of truth,
its honesty revealed,
its solemnity intricately woven into history.

Wrap yourselves in the rough hessian of righteousness,
protective against evil,
its coarseness niggling the loose strands of our conscience.

Put on the underlying cotton of justice and peace,
proclaiming the gospel,
its simplicity belying the struggle of its harsh reality.

Shroud yourselves with the flowing muslin of faith,
alive and dancing,
its mysterious shadows enticing us to future possibilities.

Adorn yourselves with the rich velvet of wisdom,
wholeness engulfing,
its myriad of tones and hues adding depth to life.

Bedeck yourselves with the fine satin of the Spirit,
revealing the word of God,
its delicate ripples expanding our horizons.

Benediction

Go from here clothed in God's rich tapestry of textures;
draped in the costly silk of truth,
proclaiming the gospel of justice and peace.
Go from here ready to expand your horizons;
adorned in the rich velvet of wisdom
and alive to the future possibilities of faith.

Villages of the Dogon people in Mali are built in such a way as to represent the human body. The Millet stores of the community are arranged around the central market places, representing the stomach of the village. At the 'head' of the village, the highest point, is the place for settling village disputes.

Mali is one of the five poorest countries in the world. The average income per person per year is £193 whilst each person owes £178 per year in international debt.

pray with partner churches in Mali.

Ages of Love

Read   Song of Songs 2.8-13; Psalm 45.1-2, 6-9

Voice 1
*The rain is over and gone,
the flowers appear on the earth,
the time for singing has come,
the voice of the turtle dove
is heard in our land.*

Voice 2
God-of-the-graffitied-love,
caught up in the swirl of emotions,
help us in the confused excitement,
the risk when conventions are flouted,
when passion engulfs our sense of reality.

God-of-the-familiar-love,
standing firm in the midst of uncertainty,
bless the silent communication
that shares another's pain,
yet understands the need to stand alone.

God-of-love-let-go,
embedded in the beauty of shared memories,
God, share with us in the presence of echoes,
the fading of struggles on which our love was built,
for love knows no time.

Voice 1
*The rain is over and gone,
the flowers appear on the earth,
the time for singing has come,
the voice of the turtle dove
is heard in our land.*

12 after Pentecost

Meditation on a mange-tout pea

What do you see in this small green vegetable?
A restaurant delicacy, all very nouvelle cuisine?
A famine infested pea steam rolled flat for weight-watchers?

Each pea tells a story:
grown from Zimbabwe to Guatemala,
but not eaten by the locals.
These cash crops are air-freighted to European markets
in the name of 'economic restructuring'.

Not grown for flavour, just for looks.
Not grown for nutrition, just for cash.
Not grown for people, just for markets.
Not grown for food, just for debt.

And eaten by us:
struggling to stand by the poor,
trying to be generous to the needy,
aiming to share with our neighbours,
wanting to be open-handed.

Even the poor grow peas for us.

Get ready to proclaim a Jubilee!
Let debts be remitted,
that all God's people might live a sweet life,
like pods bursting with ripeness.

Janet Lees

Food for thought

Invite some friends to share a vegetable supper. Collect a range of vegetables from some of the countries mentioned in this prayer handbook; as wide a range as you are able. Stir fry them together in a small amount of hot oil in a wok or other large metal pan. Add some light soy-sauce or other preferred seasoning. If possible cook them at the table naming each country represented by the ingredients. Keep the packets or labels, if any, and lay them around the table with a small candle on each one to light you meal.

---

pray for growers, exporters and importers, supermarket managers and employees and all who get vegetables on our dinner tables.

God of diversity, teach us to love our neighbours as we should love ourselves.
Now is the time for us to embrace all-comers in your name!

God of healing, equip us to tend to the lives of those whom you would not turn away.
Now is the time for us to touch the untouchables in your name!

God of justice, force us to see the rights of the poor crushed by the crimes of the rich.
Now is the time for us to stand up and shout out in your name!

God of change, help us to give others a chance by overcoming our exclusive nature.
Now is the time for us to turn our lives upside-down in your name!

God of all time, who calls for us to put our prayers into action:
This is the time for us to act!

Now is the time to act.....

It was a Friday and there were several workmen working on a shop nearby which was obviously having extensive alterations. One man, complete with hard headgear, stood for at least five minutes reading my large poster on the front of the table and then tried to get his friend to come with him to sign the [Jubilee 2000] petition. His friend said 'No, the last time I signed anything I ended up spending seven years in the Army!'

A woman came up but having started to sign, stopped and asked me to explain a bit more. When I did she immediately crossed out her name saying that she thought it was the other way round - 'a petition to stop the UK giving so many handouts to poor countries'!

I was surprised at the number of people - probably about a quarter - who came straight up after reading the poster, and signed; they seemed to appreciate the opportunity. One or two said they had seen a programme about it on TV. I remember one person saying, 'O yes, the debt crisis'. My last signatory was an elderly woman who was pleased to have a chat, saying she came out every afternoon from Twickenham and got home for tea-time ' to get out of the house'. She signed after expressing reservations about 'governments who misused aid meant for their people'. Perhaps I should have invited her to our Tuesday afternoon fellowship.

Estelle Smith, Raleigh Road UM Church, Richmond

We need to take action. Where we see injustice we should not keep silent. We can write to newspapers of politicians. We can join with people who work for justice.

Anthea Dove

pray with partner churches in Myanmar (Burma).

Prayer of "don't understand!"

Read Mark 8.27-38

This is a prayer of personal reassurance to all of us who do not always understand! It could be read by several people - a narrator and others.

Lord, this is my prayer of "don't understand."

Lord, I don't understand why, for 2000 years,
you have taught about the great suffering the Son of Man must undergo,
to face degrading execution by elders, priests and religious teachers.
Why did you die?
> You said,
> "I lose my life
> so that others might find it."

Lord, I don't understand why, for 2000 years,
others have followed your teaching, reflected your suffering
and faced brutal torture from oppressive governments and armies.
Why should they die?
> They said,
> "we lost our lives
> so that we and others might find God."

Lord, I don't understand why, for 2000 years,
you have called out: "Follow me!
You must face your own pain and suffering."
Must I die too, Lord?
> You said,
> "I will be alongside you at all times.
> So, trust your life into my hands."

Lord, this is my prayer:
help me to understand,
as Peter eventually understood,
that as I find trust in you
so I shall not always understand "why?"

So why are we trying to address Third World Debt ?

It is not just Third World nations that are moving rapidly into apparent bankruptcy. The US now had a national debt that exceeds $5 trillion; the UK's national debt is more than £400 billion; Germany's exceeds DM600 billion. All nations carry mounting debts of such magnitude that they are clearly unpayable. The level of private and commercial debt is also spiralling. So why are we trying to address Third World debt in isolation?

Peter Challen

Question time?

What questions would you ask?

What are the outstanding issues that remain unanswered for you? However many letters you have already written about the Jubilee 2000 campaign if your questions are unanswered then there's still time to write another. In your group, or while reflecting on your own, make a list of the unanswered questions about world debt that you would like answers to.

Who could best answer your questions? If they are about
- government policy then address them to the Prime Minister, the Treasury or the Minister for Overseas Development,
- local debt and social justice then address them to your MP or local community action group,
- international issues of trade and aid then write to the Christian Council for Monetary Justice or Christian Aid for more information.

Share what you know and what you still want to know. Find out what is being done to ease local debt burdens; credit unions and local co-operative and fair trading schemes.

---

pray with those working in debt relief programmes, in microcredit, in credit unions and in the IMF and all forms of banking.

Read   **Mark 9.30-37**

This prayer shows how God upsets our expectations and turns our lives upside down. The language is also unexpected, to hopefully appeal to children and adults alike It would be probably be more effective if one verse was read by a child and the other by an adult.

**Big hug
to the God of upsidedowness!
Greatest to least
and leastest is great!**
> Big God,
> you showed us
> a small child,
> to upset our set-ups,
> to make us less big,
> to show us the childishness of a 'grown-up' world:
> selfish and bickering; boring and lifeless.

**Big hug
to the God of upsidedowness!
Greatest to least
and leastest is great!**
> Big God,
> you come
> small as a child,
> to stand in our middle,
> to make us less small,
> to show us the childlikeness of your Kingdom:
> open-handed and loving; playful and dazzling.

**Big hug
to the God of upsidedowness!
Greatest to least
and leastest is great!**
> Big God
> your hugs show us
> that size isn't everything!

Ramakrishna is a determined 16 year old whose philosophy has brought him this far and will undoubtedly carry him through his promising future. He was affected by polio at the age of 2 years and was left with paralysis in both legs. At that time, in his home village in South India, there were no services for people with disabilities. So, his condition worsened as his legs became twisted and stiff. Ramakrishna was 10 years old when he came to Samarthya. Samarthya is a Sanskrit word meaning 'potential'. It is a community based rehabilitation programme working with people with disabilities based in north-east Karnataka, South India. It works across 85 villages with over 500 children and adults and provides the only service for disabled people in the area.

Following a combination of physiotherapy, surgery, sheer grit and determination, he now walks two kilometres to school where he has just completed his school leaving examinations. The next step is college.

Ramakrishna says; 'Unlike earlier, I have a standing now and can manage my life on my own. I intend to study further. I will not let anything deter me. Hope, not frustration is the key to improvement !'

Ruth Duncan

 pray with partner churches in South India.

When we lie unrested, snared in night-time, our active minds untying unwanted clutter
The Lord is on our side, settling these concerns with the tender reach of morning glow.

When voices are gagged by the smothering hands of our oppressors
The Lord is on our side, parting tied wrists.

When our angry hearts shout words that shelter our insecurities
The Lord is on our side, challenging our vision.

When our heart trembles because we are confused, our mouths too dry to share scattered thoughts
The Lord is on our side, making sense of the silence.

When our enemies kindle anger and batter our weakness
The Lord is on our side, soothing our bruises and numbing raging scars.

When we are alone or just cannot hear the breath of a loving parent
The Lord is on our side, encircling our experiences.

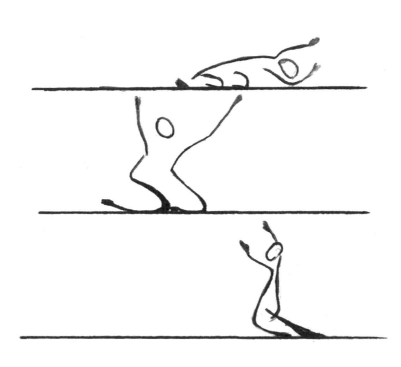

 pray with partner churches in Malaysia.

Remember the child in me, Lord?
I find it difficult to recall my own big ideas in small words,
to picture tired curls on a flopped head,
stroking a cheek made grubby by tumbles in the mud.

Something as simple as a balloon became the orb carrying my tightly
packed dreams.
I felt cheated by the bang that sprinkled them out of the reach of
spidery fingers.
The injustice make me cry at least until tea-time.

I used to skip and run,
fuelling my body with more energy than I could manage.
So I fell, nursing my wounds with trembling hands, watered by a flush
of tears.

This little person, scared of the dark,
thinking that beauty was the glitter of stars,
pulling the arm hand of a defiant grown-up down the road,
or reflecting smiles in Christmas tree lights.

The Kingdom of Heaven belongs to such as these:
to inquisitive hands that might break what they touch,
to the loud whispers that are hushed because they speak startling
truth,
to the thinking minds that demand explanations
and trust passionately that an adult will be honest with them.
Parent God, you promised the kingdom to young hearts
that sense injustice and challenge the world to be fair.
We are your children.
Your kingdom is found in excited wide-eyed chatter and a child's
voice singing.

Our large family was typical in Somalia, where the average woman has seven children. Children are looked at as the future old-age pension for the elders, as they will take care of the parents when they grow old.

Part of the reason for large families, other than lack of birth control, is that the more people who share the work, the easier life is. Even basic functions such as having water - not plenty of water, or enough water, but any water at all - required back-breaking work. Sometimes the job (of finding water) fell to me. I'd walk for days, however long it took to find water, because there was no point in coming back without it. We knew never to come home empty-handed, because then there was no hope. We had to keep going until we found something.

Waris Dirie

The No 1 casualty of Third World debt has almost disappeared...

Jubilee 2000

pray with partner churches in Somalia.

Read   **Mark 10.17-31; Hebrews 4.12-16**

'Everything is possible for you God';
we hear ourselves say in shaky words, like a child's first steps.
words that commit, with no escape clauses in the small print.
There is comfort in ownership,
a fulfilment that helps to secure us until our reluctant pockets are
nudged to share.
Reluctant, not because we do not care,
but because we fear total exhaustion
of giving more of ourselves than we can manage.
We worry that our dreams will become a misshapen web
of 'I wants, I deserve, I need'.
We lose vision of your plans for the earth and the people who live here.
Lord we pray that we may be willing and thoughtful givers
knowing that what we selflessly offer can lay foundations for the
unglittered kingdom.

'Everything is possible for you God';
words we hear ourselves say without knowing how to fulfil them,
words that require sensitivity as well as an enthusiastic heart,
because it is hard sometimes to accept what is given in love.
There is a worry that gifts exchanged between fingers and a cupped palm
can create a hand that beckons and suppresses the taker.
Proud hearts that wish to be self reliant,
feel desperate and alone in their dependence.
We worry that our dreams will become a tangled mesh
of 'please, help, I don't know where to turn'.
We lose the vision of your plans for the earth and the people who live here.
Lord we pray that we may have the courage to accept gifts freely shared
and be reminded that these are your hands offering us the love of Christ
and embracing us as part of your family:
people of the unglittered Kingdom

New life for guns

In Mozambique, there is a special project where people can bring in guns, ammunition, and all types of weapons and in return they are given a garden tool - spade, shovel, hoe .... or even a bike! There have been so many weapons brought in, everyone is really pleased. The project has been organised by the Christian Council of Mozambique. Most of the weapons have been destroyed but some have been made into sculptures! The art works are being put in public places as a statement of peace.

Rainbow, JMA Magazine, Methodist Church

The Kajiado project, in Kenya, aims to relieve women from strenuous and time-consuming jobs such as carrying water and wood. They have shown that, contrary to Maasai tradition, women can own and use donkeys to improve their livelihoods thanks to an Intermediate Technology initiated group-savings scheme and a 'merry-go-round' system of helping each other acquire donkeys. And in western Kenya, IT is now looking at ways of strengthening entrepreneurship and improving lives even further, by forging better links between the producers and the users of transport equipment. The project is also being expanded to help address transport problems of women potters, and to introduce a bicycle ambulance.

IT Matters (Intermediate Technology leaflet)

pray for the work of Intermediate Technology.

Read   Psalm 104.1-9, 24, 35c; Mark 10.35-45

Do we really know what it is we are asking?
Did we completely miss the point
  when Jesus put the little child in our midst,
or blessed the group of children
  who otherwise seemed a nuisance,
or confronted the rich man
  with the need to break with his possessions?
Are our minds so closed to Jesus' words
  about the risks of what following him will mean?

Great God,
forgive our narrowness of thinking
that keeps you small and domesticated,
a predictable and private God,
that seeks to turn your promise and power
to our own advantage.
Forgive our blinkered understanding
of the gospel of your greatness,
where there is no preferential treatment
simply because we believe;
where your good news is intended especially
for those who live outside our comfortable community.
Enlarge our vision of your kingdom in which
we shall readily drink the cup with its bitter taste
and eagerly risk being ransomed,
so that the church becomes daring and dangerous
in its seeking and serving.
Jesus said: whoever wants to be great must be your servant,
and whoever wants to be first must be the slave of all.
For the Son of Man did not come to be served but to serve,
and to give his life as a ransom for many.

 pray with partner churches in Singapore.

Read **Jeremiah 31. 7-9; Mark 10. 46-52,**

Take pity on me;
every blink is hell, antibiotics cost an arm and a leg.

Take pity on me;
seven kilometres to the clinic with little hope of getting there in
time.

Take pity on me;
both legs lost to a land mine left over from a conflict decades old.

Take pity on me;
electricity cut off again, no more 'social' until next week.

We see what we must do;
restore sight, health, dignity and hope.
My old glasses went to Bosnia
where they are now perched on
someone else's nose.

Liberating Christ
We sing for joy!
Through the priesthood of solidarity
you continue to gather your scattered people.

Sightsavers

Worldwide, 45 million people are blind. Around 80% of this blindness is needless - it could be prevented or cured. In addition, around 135 million people have low vision. 90% of the world's blind people live in developing countries. More people are blind in India than in any other country. The leading cause of blindness is cataract. There are at least 20 million people blind with cataract, which is almost always curable. Trachoma is the leading cause of preventable blindness, affecting 150 million people. The global economic burden of blindness is around £15.5 billion per year.

Trachoma is related to living standards and hygiene in a community. Lack of water, crowding and unsanitary conditions all contribute to the spread and intensity of the disease which can be treated with surgery to the eyelids, antibiotics and improved eye hygiene.

In the Zonyigiri village in Mali, 89 out of a population of 250 are blind; many of them have lost their livelihoods and all of them are dependant to some degree on the remaining sighted members of the community. Poverty can spiral in these circumstances, and the productivity of the village will nosedive as more time is spent caring for those out of action than farming the land.

Although sight is so precious, there are 35 million blind people in the world who could see. Vision 2020 is an initiative that aims to eradicate avoidable blindness by 2020.

Sight Savers International

Most HIPC's spend more on debt repayments than on the community health care than can prevent avoidable blindness.

pray for the work of Sight Savers International and the Vision 2020 campaign.

Sight Savers International is at http://www.sightsavers.org.uk

129

Read   **Deuteronomy 6.1-9, Mark 12.28-32,
Hebrews 9.11-14**

Reflect

> *Seen on a shop door:
> 'Thieves will be prosecuted'*
>
> *And me ......?
> When I bought footwear made by sweated labour;
> multicoloured sweets from multinationals;
> exotic vegetables grown to cash in on structural adjustments.
> How do these offences stock up against me ?*

Confess

> **We return to you, Holy One,
> mindful of the blood, sweat and tears
> expended by our neighbours
> to make our lives sweet.
> We ask to be forgiven.
> May we live our lives
> so that others may also live.**

Assurance of pardon

> Look what Christ has done!
> No more empty rituals.
> Rejoice! Be Happy!
> Your conscience is clear.
> Live again to serve God in your neighbourhood.

Deuteronomy 6.1-9

Psalm 119.1-8

21 after Pentecost

Hebrews 9.11-14   Mark 12.28-32

In the nitrogen-rich environment of the hi-tech hold, the 700 tonnes of bananas, cut just hours earlier in the plantations of the tiny Caribbean island of St Vincent, will be held in arrested development. When they arrive at Southampton in eight days time for the perusal of buyers from Tesco and Sainsbury's, they will emerge in the same blemish free condition in which they were loaded on the warm, breezy, night.

St Vincent is an island teetering on the edge of crisis. The banana trade, the staple of the economy is collapsing and farmers are going out of business. Official figures show that 60 per cent of the working population of St Vincent are employed in the banana industry. 70% of its agricultural exports are bananas.

Bananas are now Britain's favourite fruit and it is clear that the market is going to grow. Another problem is the standards demanded by both the EU, which in 1993 demanded tougher rules, even down to the regulation lengths for fruit, and the supermarkets, which will accept nothing less than the perfect banana. But, as one supervisor says: 'The only way we can guarantee the perfect fruit is by the greater use of pesticides'.

Christian Aid News

The Faitrade logo makes a great easy jigsaw - if only trade were such a simple puzzle. Make an even number of large F's from different coloured card and hide them around the room/worship area.

Have a hunt and get people to pair up their F's. They can exchange them for a 'prize', a small fair trade item like a nut or dried fruit, if they can name a widely available fairtrade product. Hang the F's up around the room or worship area at the end of the activity to remind people what to look out for when they shop.

pray with partner churches in Guyana.

What should I give?

I am neither scribe nor poor widow
and neither am I shepherd or wise man.
> **Lord, what should I give?**

I have so much compared to many
and so little compared to some.
> **Lord, what should I give?**

Talking religion at work is a no-no
and most of my friends go to church.
> **Lord, what should I give?**

I help with the door-to-door collections
and make coffee after the service.
> **Lord, what should I give?**

I am nice to people who don't like me
and respect everyone the same.
> **Lord, what should I give?**

I share your word with anyone who's interested
and read my Bible everyday.
> **Lord, what should I give?**

I know I am going wrong somewhere
and, please tell me, what should I give?
> **Lord, what should I give?**

Confession is a way to speak the truth. In counselling, confession and confidentiality may become an important issue when some revelations involve social or political matters, which concern crimes and security. It is necessary for counsellors to acknowledge their limits and work under some professional protection, especially in a country where witnesses may "disappear". In Rwanda, churches, both Protestant and Catholic, have begun to recognise publicly their involvement or their silence during the genocide. In December 1996 a group of Christian Tutsi, Hutu and Europeans concerned with reconciliation in Rwanda met at Detmold in Germany. At the end of the seminar, moved by the openness of the participants and by the Holy Spirit, each ethnic group made a confession on behalf of the community they were representing. Thus, this initiative encountered several criticisms because, on the one hand, the confessions gave an incomplete image of the whole reality, and, on the other, it was declared as either naive or politically dangerous.

The whole community must share in the responsibility of what happens to its members. 'As people of Africa we are familiar with the concept of corporate responsibility for the wrong-doing of the individuals in our midst because we belong to each other'. Before the genocide, each community had a group of influential people, the 'gachacha', who dealt with local problems and conflicts. At the University of Butare, some researchers are presently studying new possibilities of reintroducing this council. Justice and reparation at community level could have a role in social therapy. In the community, people often know the perpetrators. The gachacha could deal with minor crimes and initiate creative ways to provide houses, roofs and cattle to those who have lost everything. Social justice should particularly focus on poor people, but it should make sure also that women, old survivors, as well as orphans, non-accompanied children and street-kids may receive basic human rights. These issues are major challenges for community mental health.

Evelyne Burkhard

Pray for partner churches in Rwanda, and the work of reconciliation.

Read **Mark 13.7 - 8**

We have heard of the wars, seen the nations rise against nation.
As the millennium closes, our memories are full of a decade of images:
War in...

We have heard of the earthquakes, seen the famines.
As the millennium closes, our memories are full of a decade of images:
Earthquakes in...
Famine in...
Floods in...
Hurricanes in...
Volcanic eruptions...

[LEAVE TIMES OF SILENCE FOR APPROPRIATE EXAMPLES TO BE ADDED]

As we look forward to the glory of your Kingdom
don't let us become desensitised to the continuing troubles in our world.

As we look forward to the glory of your kingdom
we give thanks for the love that surrounds us
and the healing comfort you bring.

Our heavenly Father, may the rulers of the earth come together and settle the world's quarrels. Teach the people of the earth to live in peace and to love one another, following the example of Jesus Christ.

Prayer from Zaire, now the Democratic Republic of Congo

 pray with partner churches working in areas of ethnic conflict.

Read   **Psalm 93.1**

Robed in majesty:
robed in the shirt from a labourer's back,
robed in the bandage from a wounded head,
robed with the handkerchief from a widow's grasp.
   Lord, robe us in your majesty.

Girded in strength:
in the strength of the single mother,
in the strength of a refugee,
in the strength of the leper.
   Lord, gird us in your strength.

Robed in majesty:
robed in swaddling clothes,
robed in a traveller's cloak,
robed in a bloodstained shroud.
   Lord, robe us in your majesty.

Girded in strength:
in the strength of a baby's cry,
in the strength of a preacher's tongue,
in the strength of the condemned man.
   Lord, gird us in your strength.

They think it's all over......

The year 2000 is not yet over and neither is the Jubilee 2000 campaign. Whatever has happened since this book went to press there are still poor countries with high burdens of debt. Even those who have had debt reduced will need international support to develop their health and education services in the years ahead. In your group, or in a time of personal reflection, make some simple flower shapes in different coloured paper. Each one should represent something you think has been achieved or gained so far by the Jubilee 2000 campaign. Fix your flowers to a bare twig held in a small pot of earth, as a centre piece for your worship or meditation.

 pray with the staff of CWM.

Contributors

Chris Campbell is an undergraduate at Warwick University. *26, 32*

Ed Cox is a research officer with Manchester Community Pride, an ecumenical initiative working alongside churches and community groups to tackle poverty and social exclusion in Manchester.
8, 9, 11, 21, 23, 92, 94, 96, 98

Colin Ferguson represents the Doctrine Prayer and Worship Committee of the URC on the Prayer Handbook Committee.
82, 84

Melanie Frew is a public sector accountant working for the Further Education Funding Council.
24, 28, 30, 34, 36, 38, 40, 42, 78, 80, 86, 88, 132, 134, 136

Nicola Furley-Smith is a URC minister and current chair of the Prayer Handbook Committee.
90, 126

Rebecca Latham is a graduate in Fine Art from Staffordshire University. *19, 61, 63, 65, 67, 69, 71, 73, 101, 121, 127, 135*

Janet Lees is a URC minister in Sheffield and a speech therapist.
1-7, 26, 32, 89, 113, 128, 130

Tim Lowe is a URC minister and chaplain to FURY Council.
16, 44, 48, 52, 114, 116, 118

Clare McBeath is training for ministry with the Baptist Church with the Partnership for Theological Education, Manchester, and a research degree in eco-justice and feminism.
8, 12, 14, 18, 20, 22-23, 77, 100-102, 104, 106, 108, 110, 112

Alan Paterson has, for a number of years, represented the Scottish Congregational Church on the Prayer Handbook Committee.
74, 76

Becky Slow is a newly-qualified secondary school teacher of Religious Studies and English.
46, 50, 54, 56, 120, 122, 124

Andrew Stuart is a member of New Malden URC; unemployed with no formal educational qualification he expresses himself with a 'talking computer' called 'Liberator' and is learning how to live independently.
60, 62, 64, 66, 68, 70, 72

Jill Thornton is training for the ministry with the URC at Northern College, and has a particular interest in drama and art.
8-11, 13, 15, 22, 93, 94, 97, 99, 103, 104, 107, 137

Work by several members of the group is on pages *10* and *13*.

ACKNOWLEDGEMENTS

Christmas 1 - 26 December
Extract from "Old People" (Advent BBC Radio Talk) by John L Bell
Copyright © WGRG, Iona Community, Glasgow G51 3UU, Scotland

Epiphany - 6 January
1 'Three Wise Women' by Janet Lees from *Silence in Heaven*
  ed Heather Walton & Susan Durber, SCM Press 1994,
  used by permission
2 *Forever in your Debt: eight poor nations and the G8*
  published by Christian Aid

Epiphany 1 - 9 January
1 *Faith Atlas: Africa* by the Methodist Relief and Development Fund.
  Used by permission
2 *Forever in your Debt: eight poor nations and the G8*
  published by Christian Aid

Epiphany 2 - 16 January
  Forever in your Debt: eight poor nations and the G8
  published by Christian Aid

Epiphany 3 - 23 January
1 'Children Labour Under Ignorance' by Owen Bowcott (4/11/97),
  reproduced by permission of The Guardian
2 *Faith Atlas: Bangladesh* by the Methodist Relief and Development
  Fund. Used by permission

Epiphany 4 - 30 January
  Forever in your Debt: eight poor nations and the G8
  published by Christian Aid

Epiphany 5 - 6 February
  Forever in your Debt: eight poor nations and the G8
  published by Christian Aid

Epiphany 6 - 13 February
  Forever in your Debt: eight poor nations and the G8
  published by Christian Aid

Epiphany 7 - 20 February

Both from *Forever in your Debt: eight poor nations and the G8* published by Christian Aid

Epiphany 8 - 27 February

1 'Wind of Change' by Gareth Richards & John Vidal (18/11/98), reproduced by permission of The Guardian
2 *Forever in your Debt: eight poor nations and the G8* published by Christian Aid

Lent 1 - 12 March

1 *Sharing the Word through the Liturgical Year* by Gustavo Gutierrez, published by Orbis Books 1998, used by permission
2 'Jesus, master of initiation' by Anselme Sanon in *Faces of Jesus in Africa* ed Robert Schreiter, SCM Press 1992, used by permission

Lent 2 - 19 March

Chung Hyun Kyung, 'Who is Jesus for Asian Women?' in *Asian Faces of Jesus* ed R S Sugirtharajah, SCM Press 1993, used by permission

Lent 3 - 26 March

Both from *Jesus is Tricky and God is Undemocratic: the kin-dom of God in Amawoti Pitermaritzburg*, Cluster Publications. Permission sought

Lent 4 - 2 April

Both from 'An African Woman's Experience' in *Faces of Jesus in Africa* ed Robert Schreiter, SCM Press 1992, used by permission

Lent 5 - 9 April

From 'Grieving in a multi-faith society' in *Gospel from the City* by Rowland and Vincent, used by permission of the Urban Theology Unit, Sheffield

Holy Week Prayer Pilgrimage

Vicki Terrell, used by permission

Holy Thursday - 20 April
Vicki Terrell, used by permission

Holy Saturday - 22 April
Vicki Terrell, used by permission
Easter Day - 23 April
Vicki Terrell, used by permission

Easter 2 - 30 April
from the Ordinary Share Account Brochure 1999.
Used by permission of Shared Interest

Easter 5 - 21 May
Marie Stopes International (in association with the Guardian
Development Department). Used by permission

Ascension - 1 June
Christian Aid News, Issue 5, April-July 1999

Easter 7 - 4 June
from the Ordinary Share Account Brochure 1999.
Used by permission of Shared Interest

Pentecost - 11 June
Christian Aid, *Dear Life,* page 115

Trinity - 18 June
Christian Aid, *Dear Life*, page 105

4 after Pentecost - 9 July
© Katrina Mclean from *Wisdom is Calling*
published by SCM Canterbury Press. Used by permission

8 after Pentecost - 6 August
Christian Aid (Christian Aid News, Spring 1999)

13 after Pentecost - 10 September
Estelle Smith, Raleigh Road Meth/URC Church, Richmond.
Used by permission

14 after Pentecost - 17 September
Peter Challen, IM Agenda, April 1999. Used by permission

15 after Pentecost - 24 September
Ruth Duncan, © Samuha, Bangalore, India, from *Wisdom is Calling,*
published by SCM Canterbury Press. Used by permission

17 after Pentecost - 8 October
1 from *Desert Flower* by Waris Dirie, published by Virago Press 1999
2 Jubilee 2000. Used by permission

18 after Pentecost - 15 October
1 Rainbow, JMA Magazine, Methodist Church (Spring 1999).
   Used by permission
2 IT Matters (Intermediate Technology leaflet) reprinted by permission
   of The Schumacher Centre for Technology and Development

20 after Pentecost - 29 October
Sight Savers International (in association with The Guardian
Development Department). Used by permission

21 after Pentecost - 5 November
From 'The fruit trade that turned sour' by Louise Jury (5/5/98),
reproduced by permission of The Independent

22 after Pentecost - 12 November
Evelyne Burkhard, Milton Keynes and Malvern Papers on
Contemporary Society, December 1998, Edited by Revd
John Reader. Used by permission

23 after Pentecost - 19 November
From the *World at One in Prayer*, compiled by Danile Johnson
Fleming published by Harper & Row. Permission sought